A TEXTBOOK OF

HORSESHOEING

for Horseshoers and Veterinarians

by

A. Lungwitz

and

John W. Adams

Oregon State University Press
Corvallis, Oregon

THIS FACSIMILE EDITION IS PUBLISHED WITH THE PERMISSION
OF THE J. B. LIPPINCOTT COMPANY

LIBRARY OF CONGRESS CARD CATALOG NUMBER: 66-28443
LITHOGRAPHED IN THE UNITED STATES OF AMERICA

PREFACE TO FACSIMILE EDITION

IN THIS AGE of mass production and ready-made equipment, no one yet has discovered a means of adequately shoeing a horse without the services of a farrier who forms each shoe to fit the individual foot of the horse. Veterinarians have long agreed that much can be done to protect and preserve the effectiveness of a horse and to correct defects by proper shoeing. With the growing horse population and shortage of experienced farriers, a demand has arisen for materials to assist the horse owner and apprentice farrier in understanding the basic principles of the anatomy of the horse as they apply to shoeing, of the design of shoes, and of the care of hooves. This classic textbook on the subject is being reprinted at this time to meet this demand.

Professor Anton Lungwitz, a member of the Royal Saxon Veterinary Commission, instructor in the theory and practice of horseshoeing, and Director of the shoeing school of the Royal Veterinary College in Dresden, Germany, published the first edition of his now-famous manual on horseshoeing in 1884. It went through many revisions and reprintings in German. Faculty in the Veterinary School at the University of Pennsylvania found this text very useful. In 1897, Dr. John W. Adams, professor of surgery and obstetrics and lecturer on shoeing at the University of Pennsylvania, translated the eighth German edition into English and the J. B. Lippincott Company of Philadelphia published it. As new, improved editions appeared in Germany, Dr. Adams translated two more of them, the tenth edition in 1904 and the eleventh edition in 1913. The 1897 edition has 149 illustrations, the 1904 edition 160 illustrations, and the eleventh 229 illustrations.

Except for the title page and this Preface, the text presented here in facsimile reproduction is from the eleventh edition. The art work is all from that edition except that in the multi-color illustrations minor retouching has been accomplished in adapting it to modern printing methods.

On the following pages Professor Lungwitz' preface to the first edition and Professor Adams' comments on the first and second English editions are reproduced as they appear in the eleventh edition.

CORVALLIS, OREGON.

PREFACE TO THE FIRST EDITION.

THE inauguration of the law requiring horseshoers to be examined emphasizes the need of a brief and easily understood text-book on theoretical and practical horseshoeing. At the request of the *Royal Veterinary Commission,* in charge of the Royal Veterinary School in Dresden, and many interested individuals, I have attempted to meet this need by condensing within the narrowest possible limits all that is essential to the horseshoer in the practice of his profession. The subject-matter has been cast into a logically arranged course of instruction; all that is superfluous and is found only in exhaustive treatises on shoeing has been omitted.

In order to make this elementary text-book more easy to understand, numerous instructive illustrations have been incorporated, which were taken partly from " Der Fuss des Pferdes," by Leisering & Hartmann, fifth edition, Dresden, 1882; partly from the journal *Der Hufschmied,* and partly from drawings made specially for this work.

With the desire that this little book may find many friends and supply them with valuable information, it is herewith given to the public.

A. LUNGWITZ.

DRESDEN, September, 1884.

TRANSLATOR'S PREFACE.

During the past nine years in which it has been my privilege to teach horseshoeing to students of veterinary medicine in the University of Pennsylvania, and to classes of horseshoers under the auspices of the Master Horseshoers' National Protective Association of America, I have been forcibly impressed with the urgent need of a text-book of horseshoeing that is adapted to the needs of beginners. In my opinion, such a work must present a detailed description of the anatomy and physiology of the legs below the middle of the cannons, and must emphasize in unmistakable terms the definite relations which exist between certain well-defined forms of the hoof and certain well-defined standing positions of the limb. Only on this sure foundation can a thoroughly scientific system of shoeing be based. Furthermore, the teachings must be eminently practical, logically arranged, as brief as is consistent with clearness, easy of comprehension by persons who are unfamiliar with technical language, profusely illustrated, and moderate in price.

Through the kindness of my respected friend and former teacher, Professor A. Lungwitz, one of the highest authorities in all matters pertaining to shoeing, and for many years a teacher in and the Director of what I believe to be the best school of shoeing in the world, I am enabled to present to the public this translation of his text-book for students of shoeing. Written to meet requirements identical with those existing to-day in the United States, and in scope and arrangement exactly suited to both student and teacher, I am confident that it will meet the favor that it merits.

The Translator.

Philadelphia, 1904.

6

PREFACE TO THE ELEVENTH EDITION.

Since the publication in 1904 of a translation of the tenth edition of *Der Lehrmeister im Hufbeschlag,* Prof. Anton Lungwitz, the author, having reached the age of retirement has withdrawn from the activities of the *Royal Saxon Shoeing School,* and has expressed a desire that the translator assume entire responsibility for future editions.

To note the progress of farriery during the past ten years many chapters have been revised, necessitating resetting, and sixty-nine new illustrations have been added and many redrawn. It has seemed desirable to discuss the effect of weight in the shoe in altering the flight of the foot; to consider rubber pads so widely used in the United States, and to direct attention to many innovations of more or less value, that have appeared during recent years.

In preparing this edition I have had the cordial co-operation of the publishers, to whom I hereby express deepest gratitude. I wish also to record my appreciation for the many suggestions and other aid given me by Mr. Franz Enge, Chief Farrier of the shoeing shop of the Veterinary Hospital, University of Pennsylvania.　　　　　　　JOHN W. ADAMS.

UNIVERSITY OF PENNSYLVANIA, April, 1913.

CONTENTS.

CHAPTER II.

THE FOOT IN ITS RELATION TO THE ENTIRE LIMB.

PART II.

CHAPTER III.

SHOEING HEALTHY HOOFS.

CHAPTER IV.

SHOEING HORSES THAT FORGE AND INTERFERE.

CHAPTER V.

WINTER SHOEING.

CHAPTER VI.

HOOF NURTURE.

PART III.

CHAPTER VII.

GENERAL REMARKS CONCERNING THE SHOEING OF DEFECTIVE HOOFS AND LAME
HORSES.

CHAPTER VIII.

INFLAMMATIONS OF THE PODODERM (PODODERMATITIS).

CHAPTER IX.

DEFECTS OF THE HOOF.

CHAPTER X.

SHOEING MULES, ASSES, AND OXEN.

INTRODUCTION.

HORSESHOEING is an industry which requires, in equal degree, knowledge and skill.

The word " horseshoeing " embraces various acts, especially preparing the iron sole, the horseshoe; forming it and fitting it to the hoof, whose ground-surface has been previously dressed in accordance with the direction of the limb, and fastening it to the hoof by means of nails.

Owing to the complicated structure of the hoof, success in the practice of horseshoeing requires a knowledge of the anatomy and physiology of the horse's body in general and of the foot in particular.

The object of shoeing is,—

1. To protect the hoof from excessive wear, and thus render the horse continuously serviceable upon our hard roads.

2. To prevent slipping and falling during the winter season.

3. To so far remove the disadvantages of faulty positions of the limbs that horses may render good service, and, in some cases,

4. To cure or improve diseased or defective hoofs or feet.

Horseshoeing, though apparently simple, involves many difficulties, owing to the fact that the hoof is not an unchanging body, but varies much with respect to form, growth, quality, and elasticity. Furthermore, there are such great differences in the character of ground-surfaces and in the nature of horses' work that shoeing which is not performed with great ability and care induces disease and makes horses lame.

13

In view of these facts, a thorough training of the young horseshoer in the principles and practice of his trade is not only greatly to be desired, but is really essential to success; unreasoning work does as much harm in this as in any other vocation. *A good common-school education is necessary* (more will do no harm). Further requisites are a *healthy body*, not too tall, *liking for the work, aptness,* an active, *reasoning mind, fearlessness, dexterity, a good eye for proportion,* and, finally, *careful selection of a master-instructor.* Theoretically educated, practically experienced and approved masters, in whose shops all kinds of horses are shod, are to be preferred.

During his term of apprenticeship the young apprentice should *learn to make drawings of horseshoes, of tools of the trade,* and of hoofs of various forms, and should also make *one or more model shoes as an indication of his ability.* After completing his time he should seek a position in a first-class shop, either at home or abroad. A visit to foreign lands will widen one's mental horizon and make him a broader, abler man in every respect. Later, opportunity will be given to some (in Germany) to join the cavalry, and thus acquire a good education in shoeing under the patronage of the government. Finally, a course of instruction in a school of horseshoeing will convert an already practical and intelligent horseshoer into a thoughtful, capable, expert workman.

The scope of horseshoeing is by no means so narrow and insignificant as it may appear, and since a knowledge of the anatomy and physiology of the horse's body in general, and of the foot in particular, is necessary, it is evident that the schools of horseshoeing in which one can get the best instruction are those in which there is not only a regularly graded course of instruction, with demonstrations upon dissected material and upon living horses, but also an abundance of daily work at the forge and on the floor in the shoeing of horses. A **course of four to six weeks is not sufficient.**

Furthermore, it should be borne in mind that schools of horseshoeing are not for the purpose of instructing young men in all matters which pertain to the trade, but only in the making of shoes, the critical examination and management of hoofs, and the rational and skilful performance of shoeing. For this reason it is not advisable for young men to attend a school of horse-shoeing until they have at least completed their apprenticeship.

HORSESHOEING.

PART I.

CHAPTER I.

THE GROSS ANATOMY OF THE HORSE.

THE supporting structure of the horse's body is the **bony framework** or skeleton (Fig. 1, page 18). We distinguish in the skeleton the bones of the head, trunk, and limbs.

The **bones of the head** are numerous and, excepting the lower jaw, are solidly united with one another. In general, we distinguish in the head only the upper and lower jaws (1 and 1′). Both form various cavities; for example, the cranial cavity, in which the brain lies, the orbital cavities (eye-sockets), the nasal passages, and the mouth. Besides, the teeth are set in the jaws.

The **trunk** comprises the bones of the spinal column, thorax, and pelvis.

The *spinal* or *vertebral column* (2 to 6), which bears the head at its anterior end, is the chief support of the entire skeleton. It consists of from fifty-two to fifty-four single and irregular bones called vertebræ, placed in the upper part of the median vertical plane of the body. Each vertebra, with the exception of those of the tail (coccygeal or caudal vertebræ), is traversed by a large opening called the vertebral foramen. The vertebræ are placed end to end in a row, and through them runs a continuous large canal called the *vertebral* or *spinal canal,* in which lies the spinal cord. The horse has seven cervical, eighteen dorsal, six lumbar, five sacral, and sixteen to eighteen caudal vertebræ. The sacral vertebræ are grown together to form one piece called the sacrum.

FIG. 1.

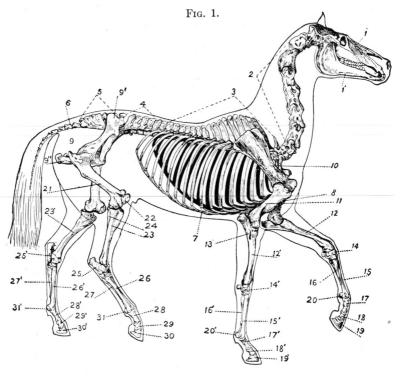

SKELETON OF THE HORSE.—1, bones of the head; 1′, lower jaw; 2, cervical vertebræ; 3, dorsal vertebræ; 4, lumbar vertebræ; 5, sacral vertebræ (sacrum); 6, coccygeal vertebræ; 7, ribs; 8, sternum (breast-bone); 9, pelvis; 9′, ilium; 9″, ischium; 10, scapula (shoulder-blade); 11, humerus; 12, radius; 13, ulna; 14, carpus (knee); 15, large metacarpal bone (cannon); 16, rudimentary metacarpal bones (splint-bones); 17, os suffraginis (long pastern); 18, os coronæ (short pastern); 19, os pedis (hoof-bone); 20, sesamoid bones; 21, femur; 22, patella (knee-pan, stifle); 23, tibia; 24, fibula; 25, tarsus, or hock; 26, large metatarsal bone (cannon); 27, rudimentary metatarsals (splint bones); 28, os suffraginis (long pastern); 29, os coronæ (short pastern); 30, os pedis (hoof-bone, "coffin bone"); 31, sesamoid bones.

The *thorax* is formed by the ribs and the breast-bone or sternum. The horse has eighteen ribs on each side (7), and all articulate with the dorsal vertebræ. The first eight pairs unite by their lower ends directly to the sternum or breast-bone, and are therefore called *true ribs,* while the last ten pairs are only indirectly attached to the sternum, and are consequently called *false ribs.* The sternum (8) lies between the forelegs, and helps to form the floor of the chest cavity. The space enclosed by the bones of the thorax is called the thoracic, pulmonary, or chest cavity, and contains the heart and lungs. The *bones of the pelvis* form a complete circle or girdle. The upper part, called the ilium (9'), articulates on its inner side with the sacrum (5), while its outer side is prolonged to form a prominent angle, which is the support of the hip, and is called the " point of the hip." The posterior part of the pelvis is called the ischium (9"), and that part lying between the ilium and the ischium and forming part of the floor of the pelvis is called the pubis.

The space between the thorax and the pelvis, bounded above by the lumbar vertebræ and shut in below and on the sides by the skin and muscular walls of the belly (abdomen), is called the *abdominal cavity.* This cavity opens directly into the pelvic cavity, and contains the stomach, intestines, liver, spleen, pancreas, kidneys, and a part of the generative organs. The thoracic and abdominal cavities are separated by a muscular partition, the *diaphragm.*

The **bones of the limbs** may be likened to columns, upon which the body rests; they articulate with one another at various angles, are tubular in structure, and strong.

The bones of the **fore-limbs** *do not articulate directly with the bones of the trunk,* but are attached to the body by means of the skin and muscles. From above to below we distinguish the following bones:

1. The *scapula,* or shoulder-blade (10), a flat, triangular bone, prolonged at its upper border by a flat, very elastic cartilage, called the scapular cartilage. At its lower end the scapula articulates with—

2. The upper end of the *humerus* (11), forming the *shoulder-joint* (scapulo-humeral articulation). The humerus articulates at its lower end with—

3. The *radius* (12) and the *ulna* (13), to form the *elbow-joint*. These two bones are the basis of the *forearm*. The ulna, smaller and weaker than the radius, lies behind and projects above it to form the point of the elbow. The lower end of the radius articulates with—

4. The *carpus, or knee* (14), which comprises seven small, cubical bones disposed in two horizontal rows, one above the other. The upper row comprises four bones and the lower row three. The lower row rests upon—

5. The large metacarpal or *cannon bone,* and the two rudimentary metacarpal or *splint-bones.* The lower end of the radius, the upper ends of the metacarpal bones, and the small carpal bones together form the carpal or *knee-joint* (wrist of man). Of the metacarpals, the middle one is the largest, longest, strongest, and most important, and is called the *large metacarpal, cannon,* or *shin-bone* (15). It articulates at its lower end with the os suffraginis, or long pastern (17), and with the two small sesamoid bones (20). On each side of the upper part of its posterior surface lie the two long, slender splint-bones (16). The inner splint-bone is sometimes affected with bony thickenings (exostoses) called " splints."

6. The bones of the *phalanges* (all bones below the cannon) will be fully described in another place.

The bones of the **hind limbs** articulate *directly* with the pelvis at the hip-joint. They are stronger than the bones of the anterior limbs. We distinguish the following bones in the hind legs:

1. The highest bone in the hind limb is the *femur* (21). It is the strongest bone in the entire body. It lies in an oblique direction downward and forward, and at its lower end articulates with—

2. The *patella* (22), the *tibia* (23), and the *fibula* (24), to form the *stifle-joint* (knee of man). The patella plays over the anterior surface of the lower end of the femur. The fibula is small, and lies against the upper and outer side of the tibia. The latter at its lower end articulates with—

3. The bones of the tarsus, or *hock* (25), which are six small, irregular bones disposed in three rows, one above another. The *os calcis*, or *heel-bone*, and the *astragalus* are in the uppermost row, and are the most important. The former projects above the true hock-joint from behind, to form a long lever, the upper end of which is called the " point of the hock," and the latter articulates with the tibia. The tarsal (hock) bones articulate below with—

4. The *metatarsal bones* (26 and 27), which are longer, and the cannon narrower from side to side, than the corresponding metacarpal bones, but are otherwise similar.

5. The *phalanges* of a hind limb (28 to 31) are also narrower than those of a fore-limb, but are nearly alike in other respects.

All the horse's bones present small, but more or less distinct openings (nutrient foramina) for the passage of blood-vessels and nerves. Many bones possess roughened elevations and depressions, to which ligaments, tendons, or muscles are attached. With the exception of the os pedis, all bones are enveloped in a sort of " bone-skin " called **periosteum.** The bones unite among themselves to form either *movable* or *immovable unions.* A movable union between two or more bones is termed a " joint," or **articulation.** The articulating ends of the bones, presenting on one side a convex surface (head or condyle) and on the other a corresponding concave surface (glenoid or cotyloid cavity), are covered with elastic *articular cartilage.* The bones are bound together by means of **ligaments,** which are tough, fibrous, cord-like, or sheet-like structures. Ligaments are either (1) *capsular* or (2) *funicular* (cord-like). Every articulation in the limbs possesses a capsular ligament, and all, except the shoulder-joint, have several funicular (cord-like) ligaments. The capsular ligaments are lined upon their inner face with a delicate membrane synovial membrane) which secretes the *synovia,* or " joint water," whose function is to lubricate the joint and prevent friction; they enclose the joint in a sort of air-tight cuff or sack. The funicular ligaments are very strong and often large, and are the chief means of union of the bones. The immovable articulations are termed *sutures;* they are found principally in the head. The mixed joints are found between the bodies of the vertebræ, each two of which are united by an elastic fibro-cartilage which, in the form of a pad, lies between them, and by its elasticity allows of very slight movement, though the spinal column as a whole can execute manifold and wide movements, as shown by the neck and tail.

Joints which permit motion in all directions are known as **free joints**; such are the shoulder- and hip-joints (ball-and-socket joints). Those which admit of motion in but two directions (flexion and extension), and often to a very limited extent, are called **hinge-joints,**—*e.g.,* the elbow, hock, and fetlock. The joints between the long and short pasterns and between the latter and the pedal bone are imperfect hinge-joints, because they allow of some other movements besides flexion and extension. The articulation between the first and second cervical vertebræ (atlas and axis) is called a **pivot-joint.**

The skeleton represents a framework which closely approaches the external form of the body, and by reason of its hardness and stiffness furnishes a firm foundation for all other parts of the body. By reason of the great variety of position and direction of the bones, and of the fact that changes of position of each single part of this complicated system of levers may result in the greatest variety of bodily movements, we can readily understand how the horse is enabled to move from place to place. Of course, the bones have no power of themselves to move, but this power is possessed by other organs that are attached to the bones. These organs are the **muscles,** and, owing to their ability to contract and shorten themselves, and afterwards to relax and allow themselves to be stretched out, they furnish the motive power that is communicated to and moves the bones.

The muscles of the body massed together are the red flesh which we observe in every slaughtered animal. They are not, however, so shapeless as they appear while in this condition; on the contrary, they present well-arranged muscular layers

FIG. 2.

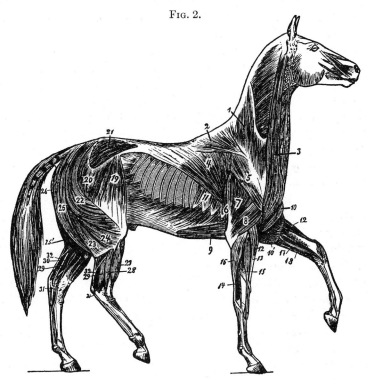

OUTER MUSCLES OF THE HORSE.—1, cervical trapezius; 2, dorsal trapezius; 3, mastoido-humeralis; 4, great dorsal muscle; 5, long abductor of the arm; 6, long extensor of the forearm; 7, large extensor of the forearm; 8, short extensor of the forearm; 9, sterno-trochinus (deep pectoral); 10, sterno-aponeuroticus; 11, great serratus; 12, common extensor of the metacarpus; 13, common extensor of the toe (anterior extensor); 14, common extensor of the long pastern (lateral extensor); 15, oblique extensor of the metacarpus; 16, external flexor of the metacarpus; 17, internal flexor of the metacarpus; 18, oblique flexor of the metacarpus; 19, fascia lata; 20, superficial gluteus (anterior portion); 21, middle gluteus; 22, superficial gluteus (posterior portion); 23 and 24, femoral biceps; 25, semitendinosus; 26, semimembranosus; 27, anterior extensor of the toe; 28, lateral extensor of the toe; 29, perforans muscle (deep flexor of toe); 30, oblique flexor of the phalanges; 31, perforatus tendon (superficial flexor of phalanges); 32, Achilles tendon (ham-string).

of variable size, thickness, length, and position. (See Fig. 2.) The muscles clothe the skeleton externally, give the body its peculiar form, and, by their special power of · contraction, change the relative positions of the bones and thus make it possible for the animal to move. For this reason, the muscles are called the **active,** and the bones the **passive,** organs of motion. By carefully examining a muscle it will be found to consist of actual, minute, reddish, *muscular fibres.* As a rule, muscles terminate in more or less strong, glistening, fibrous cords called **tendons,** or fibrous sheets termed aponeuroses, by which they are attached to the bones. In the limbs are muscles terminating in very long tendons, which act as draw-lines upon the distant bones of the foot (long and short pasterns and pedal bone) and set them in motion. Such long tendons are enclosed in sheaths of thin, membranous tissue, known as *tendon sheaths.* The inner surface of such a sheath is in direct contact with the surface of the tendon, and secretes a thin slippery fluid (synovia) which lubricates the tendon and facilitates its gliding within the sheath.

As long as the bones, articulations, muscles, and tendons of the limbs remain healthy, just so long will the legs maintain their natural direction and position. Frequently, however, this normal condition of the limbs is gradually altered by disease of the bones, joints, and tendons, and defects in the form and action of the lower parts of the limbs arise that often require attention in shoeing.

THE FOOT.

A. The Bones of the Foot.

Since the horse is useful to man only by reason of his movements, his foot deserves the most careful attention. The horseshoer should be familiar with all its parts. Fig. 3 shows the osseous framework of the foot, consisting of the lower end of the cannon bone (A), the long pastern (B), the two sesamoid bones (C), the short pastern (D), and the pedal bone (E). The lower end of the cannon, or large metacarpal bone (A) exhibits two convex articular surfaces (condyles) separated by a median ridge running from before to behind, and all covered by articular cartilage. On both the external and the internal aspects of the lower end of the cannon are small uneven depressions in which ligaments take their attachment.

The condyles of the cannon articulate with the os suffraginis (long pastern) and the two sesamoids (Figs. 3, *C,* and 4, *B*) in such a manner that in the forefeet the cannon makes an angle with the long pastern of from one hundred and thirty-five to one hundred and forty degrees, and in the hind feet of from one hundred and forty to one hundred and forty-five degrees.

The **long pastern** (first phalanx) (Fig.

Fig. 3.

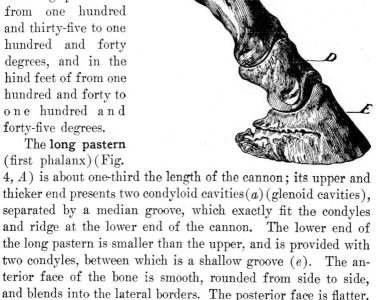

4, *A*) is about one-third the length of the cannon; its upper and thicker end presents two condyloid cavities (*a*) (glenoid cavities), separated by a median groove, which exactly fit the condyles and ridge at the lower end of the cannon. The lower end of the long pastern is smaller than the upper, and is provided with two condyles, between which is a shallow groove (*e*). The anterior face of the bone is smooth, rounded from side to side, and blends into the lateral borders. The posterior face is flatter, and shows a clearly marked triangle to which ligaments attach.

The two **sesamoid bones** (Fig. 4, *B*) are small, and somewhat pyramidal in shape, and, lying against the posterior part of the condyles of the cannon bone, increase the articular surfaces at the upper end of the long pastern.

FIG. 4.

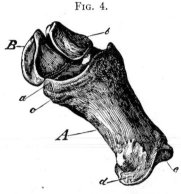

Os suffraginis with both sesamoid bones in position, as in Fig. 3. *A*, os suffraginis; *B*, sesamoid bones; *a*, upper joint-surface of long pastern; *b*, joint-surface of sesamoid bones; *c*, roughened surface at upper end; *d*, roughened surface at lower end, both for attachment of ligaments; *e*, lower joint surface.

The short pastern (second phalanx) (Figs. 5 and 6) lies under the first phalanx and above the os pedis; it is somewhat cubical in shape. Its upper articular surface (Fig. 5, *a*) presents two glenoid cavities to correspond with the condyles of the first phalanx. The lower articular surface (Fig. 5, *d*) resembles the lower end of the first phalanx. The upper posterior border of this bone is prominent and prolonged transversely (Fig. 6, *a*), to serve as a *supporting ledge* for the first phalanx,

FIG. 5.

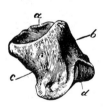

Short pastern (os coronæ) viewed in front and in profile: *a*, upper joint-surface; *b*, anterior surface; *c*, lateral surface; *d*, lower joint-surface.

FIG. 6.

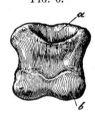

Short pastern seen from behind: *a*, smooth surface over which the perforans tendon glides; *b*, lower joint-surface.

as a point of attachment for the perforatus tendon, and as a gliding surface for the perforans tendon.

The lowest bone of the limb is the **third phalanx or os pedis** (Fig. 7). In form it is similar to the hoof. The *anterior or wall-surface* (*a*) is rough, like pumice stone. Above and in front is the *pyramidal eminence* to which the tendon of the anterior extensor of the phalanges attaches. Behind, the bone extends backward to form the *inner* and *outer branches* (*c, c*) or wings of the os pedis. The *upper,* articular surface (*b*) slopes backward and downward. The *lower,* solar or plantar surface (Fig. 8, *a*) is slightly concave, and presents posteriorly a half-moon-shaped excavation, with a roughened border called the *semilunar crest* (*c*), to which the perforans tendon attaches; just above this crest are two small holes (*e*) known as the *plantar foramina,* through which the plantar arteries pass into the bone. The surfaces of wall and sole come together in a sharp edge, which is circular in its

FIG. 7.

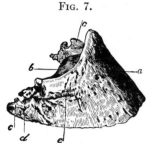

Os pedis seen in profile and in front; *a,* anterior face with pyramidal eminence above; *b,* joint-surface; *c,* wings or branches of hoof-bone; *d,* notch which, by the attachment of the lateral cartilage, is converted into a foramen and leads to *e,* the preplantar fissure.

FIG. 8.

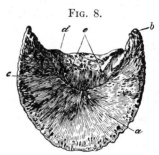

Lower surface of hoof-bone; *a,* anterior portion covered by the velvety tissue of the sole; *b,* wing of the os pedis; *c,* semilunar crest, to which the perforans tendon attaches; *d,* plantar fissure leading to *e,* plantar foramen.

course. It is easy to tell whether a pedal bone is from a fore or a hind limb; the os pedis of a hind leg has a steeper and more pointed toe, and a more strongly concaved solar surface than the same bone of a foreleg. Not only is the outline of the sharp inferior border of the os pedis of a *front foot more rounded at the toe,* but when placed on a flat surface the *toe does not touch* by reason of being turned slightly upward, much as a shoe designed to give a "rolling motion." The os pedis of a *hind foot is narrower from side to side* (pointed), and *does not turn up at the toe.*

The right and left hoof-bones are also, as a rule, easily distinguished by variations in the surfaces of wall and sole. The shape of the os pedis corresponds to the form of the horny box or hoof, and therefore a knowledge of this bone is absolutely necessary.

The **navicular bone** (os naviculare, nut-bone, Figs. 9 and 10) is an accessory or sesamoid bone to the os pedis. It is a small bone, transversely elongated and situated behind and below the os pedis and between the wings of the latter. It adds to the articular surface of the pedal joint. Its under surface is smooth, and acts as a gliding surface for the perforans tendon, which is quite wide at this point.

FIG. 9.   FIG. 10.

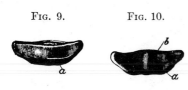

Fig. 9 represents the upper surface of the navicular bone; Fig. 10 the lower surface of the same: *a*, anterior border; *b*, slight elevation in middle of under surface.

The long axes of the three phalanges (os suffraginis, os coronæ, and os pedis) should unite to form a straight line, when viewed either from in front or from one side; that is, the direction of each of these three bones should be the same as the common direction of the three considered as a whole.

In young colts both the long and short pasterns are in three parts and the pedal bone in two parts, all of which unite later in life to form their respective single bones.

In mules and asses the os pedis is comparatively small and narrow. In cattle all three phalanges are double, and split hoofs cover the divided os pedis.

B. The Articulations of the Foot.

There are three articulations in the foot—namely, the fetlock, coronary, and pedal joints. All are hinge-joints, the fetlock being a perfect hinge-joint, and the other two imperfect hinge-joints. Each has a *capsular ligament,* and also several *funicular* or cord-like *ligaments* which are placed at the sides of (lateral ligaments), or behind (on the side of flexion) the joints.

I. The **fetlock** or **metacarpo-phalangeal articulation** is formed by the condyles at the lower end of the cannon bone and the glenoid cavities formed by the union of the articular surfaces of the sesamoids and the upper end of the first phalanx. The following ligaments are about this joint:

1. *Two lateral ligaments,* an external and an internal (Fig. 11, *a*).

2. *Two lateral sesamoid ligaments (f).*

3. An *intersesamoid ligament* (Fig. 12, *b*), a thick, fibrous m a s s , binding the sesamoid bones almost immovably together, e x t e n d i n g above them and presenting on its posterior face a smooth groove, i n which glide the flexor tendons o f t h e phalanges (perforans and perforatus).

4. The *suspensory ligament* of the fetlock (Figs. 11, *c,* 12, *c,* and 13, *c,* pages 29 and 30). This may also be called the superior sesamoid ligament. It is a long

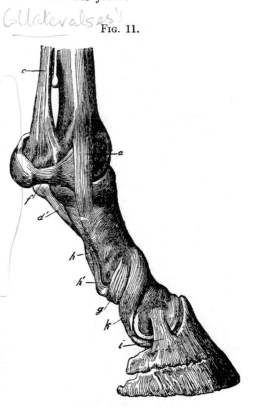

FIG. 11.

and very powerful brace, originating on the lower row of carpal bones (bones of the hock in the hind leg) and on the upper end of the cannon between the heads of the two splint-bones, and dividing at the lower third of the cannon into two branches (*c*), which are attached one to each sesamoid bone. Below these bones these two branches are prolonged obliquely downward and forward on opposite sides of the long pastern to pass into the borders of the anterior extensor tendon of the toe at about the middle of the long pastern (Fig. 14, *b*′, page 32).

FIG. 12.   FIG. 13.

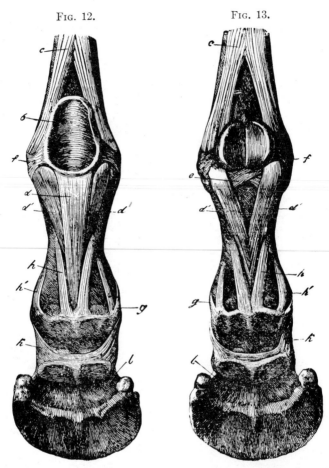

Fig. 11 shows a side view, and Figs. 12 and 13 a posterior view of the phalangeal bones, with their articular ligaments. The lettering is the same in all three figures: *a*, lateral ligament of fetlock-joint; *b*, intersesamoid ligament; *c*, suspensory ligament of the fetlock; *d*, median branch of inferior sesamoid ligament; *d'*, lateral branches of inferior sesamoid ligament; *e*, deep inferior sesamoid ligament; *f*, lateral sesamoid ligaments; *g*, inferior coronary ligaments; *h*, superior coronary ligaments; *h'*, median coronary ligaments; *i*, lateral pedal ligament; *k*, lateral coronary ligament and suspensory ligament of the navicular bone; *l*, interosseous ligament.

5. The *inferior sesamoid ligament* (Figs. 11, *d'*, 12, *d, d'*, and 13, *d', E*). This originates at the lowest part of the sesamoid bones and intersesamoid ligament, and consists of *three parts* or

branches. The *median branch* (*d*) is the longest and strongest, and takes its lower attachment in the middle of the fibro-cartilaginous lip found on the upper border of the posterior face of the second phalanx. The *two lateral branches* (*d'*) approach each other as they descend, and terminate on the sides of the roughened triangle on the posterior face of the first phalanx.

6. The *deep inferior sesamoid ligament* (Fig. 13, *e*) is quite short, and consists of a number of distinct, thin fibrous bands lying directly against the bone and entirely covered by the median and lateral inferior sesamoid ligaments. These fibrous bands cross one another in passing from the sesamoids to the first phalanx.

II. The **coronary joint** is the simplest of the three articulations of the foot. The long pastern furnishes two condyles and the short pastern two glenoid cavities. Besides a capsular ligament there are—

1. *Two lateral coronary ligaments* (*k*) and,

2. *Six posterior coronary ligaments,*—namely, *two superior* coronary ligaments (*h*), *two median* coronary ligaments (*h'*), and *two inferior* coronary ligaments (*g*).

III. The **pedal articulation** ("coffin" joint) is an imperfect hinge-joint, and is formed by the condyles at the lower end of the short pastern and the two glenoid cavities in the united upper surfaces of the pedal and navicular bones. Besides the *capsular ligament* (Figs. 12 and 13, *l*), which binds all three bones together, there are the following accessory ligaments:

1. *Two strong lateral ligaments,* an external and an internal (Fig. 11, *i*), whose posterior borders are lost in the lateral cartilages which cover them.

2. *Two lateral suspensory ligaments of the navicular bone* (*k*). They begin on the posterior border and ends of the navicular bone, and terminate on the lower part of the anterior surface of the os suffraginis, where they are lost in the lateral ligaments of the coronary articulation.

3. The *lateral ligaments of the lateral cartilages, navicular bone,* and *os pedis.* They are short, and unite the navicular bone with the os pedis and lateral cartilages.

Of the three phalangeal articulations, the pedal is the only one that permits of any lateral movement; hence it is an imperfect hinge-joint.

C. The Locomotory Organs of the Foot.

Though the muscles are the organs which produce motion, the horseshoer need concern himself only with the tendons of those muscles which extend and flex the phalanges. These **tendons** are either **extensors or flexors.** The extensors lie on the *anterior face* and the flexors on the *posterior face* of the phalanges.

The *anterior extensor of the phalanges* (Fig. 14, *a*) extends the long and short pasterns and the hoof-bone; it is broad, and made somewhat broader by receiving the branches of the suspensory ligament (*b'*) that come from the sesamoid bones. It takes a firm attachment on the pyramidal eminence of the os pedis. In the forefeet the long pastern has a special extensor tendon (*c*), which is known as the *lateral extensor*. When the muscles to which these tendons are attached act,—that is, when

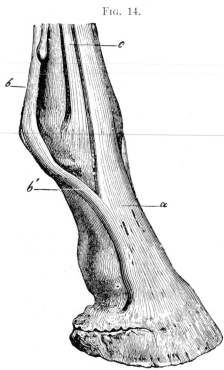

FIG. 14.

Right forefoot viewed from in front and from the external side: *a*, anterior extensor tendon of the toe; *b*, suspensory ligament of the fetlock; *b'*, branch of the same passing forward and uniting with the extensor tendon of the toe; *c*, extensor tendon of the os suffraginis (absent in the hind leg), called the lateral extensor.

they draw themselves together, or *contract,* as we term this action,—the foot is carried forward (extended).

There are *two flexor tendons* of the phalanges,—namely, the *superficial* (perforatus tendon) and the *deep* (perforans tendon).

1. The *superficial flexor* or *perforatus tendon* (Figs. 15, *b,* and 16, *a, b*) lies behind, immediately under the skin, and covers the deep flexor or perforans tendon. At the gliding surface between the sesamoid bones (Fig. 15, *f*) it broadens, and forms a ring or tube (Fig. 15, *b'*) through which the perforans tendon (*a'''*) passes, while a short distance farther down it bifurcates, or divides into two branches (Figs. 15, *b'',* and 16, *b*), which terminate, one on either side, partly on the inferior lateral borders of the first phalanx and partly on the fibro-cartilage of the second phalanx. It acts simultaneously on the long and short pasterns.

2. The *deep flexor* or *perforans*

FIG. 15.

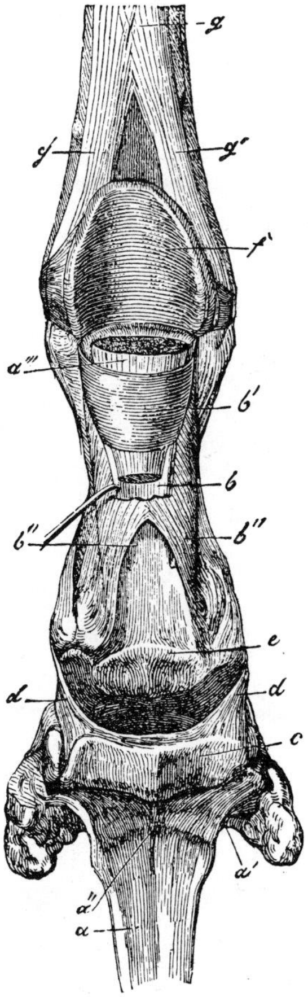

Right forefoot seen from behind: *a,* lower end of the perforans tendon, cut through and hanging down, so that its anterior surface is visible; *a',* lower expanded end (plantar aponeurosis) of this tendon, which attaches itself to the semilunar crest of the os pedis; *a'',* shallow groove which receives the slight elevation on the under surface of the navicular bone; *a''',* piece of the perforans tendon enclosed by the ring formed by the perforatus tendon; *b,* perforatus tendon bent over backward so that its anterior surface is visible; *b',* ring of the perforatus tendon; *b'',* terminal branches of the same; the perforans tendon passes through the space between these two branches; *c,* navicular bone; *d,* suspensory ligament of the same; *e,* smooth surface on the os coronæ over which the perforans tendon glides; *f,* the smooth groove (sesamoid groove) on the posterior surface of the intersesamoid ligament for the gliding of the perforans tendon; *g,* body of the suspensory ligament of the fetlock; *g',* terminal branches of the same, attaching to the sesamoid bones.

tendon (Figs. 15, *a,* and 16, *c*) is cylindrical and stronger than the perforatus tendon; above the fetlock-joint it lies between the perforatus and the suspensory liga-

FIG. 16.

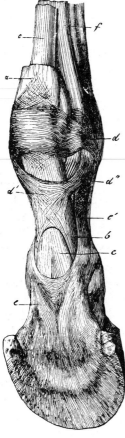

ment of the fetlock. At the sesamoid bones it passes through the ring formed by the perforatus tendon (Fig. 15, *b'*), then becomes broad and double-edged, passes between the t w o t e r m i n a l branches of the perforatus, glides over the fibro-cartilage of the second phalanx and over the inferior surface of the navicular bone, and finally ends on the semilunar crest of the third phalanx. In common with the perforatus tendon it flexes the foot.

If at a point a few inches above the fetlock a limb be cut through from behind, the knife will pass successively through the following structures: skin, perforatus tendon, perforans tendon, suspensory ligament, cannon bone, lateral extensor tendon, anterior extensor tendon, and, lastly, the skin on the anterior surface of the limb. The flexor tendons are frequently thickened and shortened by inflammation due to injury, and as a result the foot is pulled backward and the hoof gradually becomes more nearly upright,—*i.e.,* stubby, steep-toed. A knowledge of the

Right forefoot seen from behind and a little from the external side: *a,* perforatus tendon; *b,* terminal branches of the same; *c,* perforans tendon; *d,* annular ligament which attaches to the sesamoid bones: *d',* the "x" ligament, which attaches by four branches to the os suffraginis;. *d",* an upper branch of the same (the lower branches are not shown in the figure); *e,* reinforcing sheath of the perforans tendon, covering the under surface of the latter and attached by its branches at *e'* to the lower end of the os suffraginis; *f,* suspensory ligament of the fetlock.

normal condition of the tendons is, therefore, absolutely necessary to the horseshoer. Both flexor tendons are embraced and held in place by ligaments and fascia passing out from the phalanges (Figs. 16, d', and 24, e, f). The extensor and flexor tendons essentially contribute to the strong union of the phalangeal bones, and especially to the support and stability of the fetlock-joint. The gliding of the tendons is made easy by the secretion of a lubricating fluid, called synovia, from the inner surface of the sheaths which surround them. In thin-skinned well-bred horses with sound limbs one can not only distinctly feel the tendons through the skin, but can see their outline. *When the tendons and bones are free from all inflammatory thickenings, and the tendon sheaths are not visibly distended, we say that the leg is " clean."*

Mucous Bursæ and Tendon Sheaths.

Accessory to the tendons, there are in the foot roundish, membranous sacs (mucous bursæ) and membranous tubes (tendon sheaths). Both contain a liquid resembling synovia (" joint-water "), which facilitates the gliding of the tendons. These bursæ and sheaths are often distended to form soft tumors, known as hygromata (" wind-puffs," " wind-galls ").

(*a*) **Mucous Bursæ.**—They lie beneath tendons at those places where the tendons pass over bony prominences.

1. The mucous bursa of the anterior extensor tendon of the toe is about the size of a walnut, and lies between the tendon and the capsular ligament of the fetlock-joint (Figs. 17, g, and 18, e).

2. The mucous bursa of the extensor tendon of the long pastern (lateral extensor) is somewhat smaller, and lies, likewise, beneath the tendon, between it and the capsular ligament of the fetlock-joint (Fig. 17, h).

3. The mucous bursa of the navicular region lies between the under surface (gliding surface) of the navicular bone and the flexor pedis perforans tendon (deep flexor). Its width

equals the length of the navicular bone, and it extends upward and downward beyond the bone. Above, it is separated from the sheath of the perforans tendon (" great sesamoid sheath ") by a membranous partition; below, it passes to the attachment of the perforans tendon to the semilunar crest of the os pedis.

(b) There is but one tendon sheath in the foot,—the sheath common to the two flexor tendons (great sesamoid sheath). It

FIG. 17.

FIG. 18.

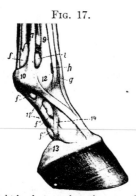

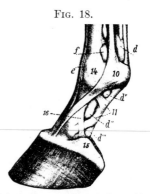

Right forefoot seen from the external side; *f, f', f'', f'''*, great sesamoid sheath (tendon-sheath); *g*, mucous bursa beneath anterior extensor tendon of the toe; *h*, mucous bursa beneath extensor tendon of long pastern; *i*, synovial distension of the fetlock-joint; 7, suspensory ligament; 9, cannon bone; 10, outer sesamoid bone; 12, fetlock-joint; 13, lateral cartilage; 14, suspensory ligament of the lateral cartilage. (Ellenberger in Leisering's Atlas and Veterinary Anatomy, Sisson, Saunders.)

Right forefoot seen from the inner side; *d, d', d'', d'''*, great sesamoid sheath; *e*, mucous bursa beneath anterior extensor tendon of the toe; *f*, synovial distension of fetlock-joint; 10, inner sesamoid bone; 11, "x" ligament; 14, fetlock-joint; 15, lateral cartilage; 16, suspensory ligament of lateral cartilage (Ellenberger in Leisering's Atlas and Veterinary Anatomy, Sisson, Saunders.)

encloses the flexor tendons from the middle third of the cannon down to the middle of the short pastern, and is intimately united with the flexor pedis perforans tendon (Fig. 17, *f, f', f'', f'''*. Fig. 18, *d, d', d'', d'''*).

Altering the Relative Tension of the Flexor Tendons and Suspensory Ligament of the Fetlock-Joint.

The body-weight imposed at the fetlock-joint is supported, in large part, by the suspensory ligament; somewhat less weight is borne by the perforans tendon, and a still smaller amount by the perforatus. The coronary joint is supported chiefly by the perforatus, assisted by the perforans. The pedal joint is pressed forward and upward by the perforans tendon passing in a curve beneath the navicular bone. Each of these three structures bears its normal proportion of the body-weight when the three phalanges, as viewed from the side, form a continuous straight line from the fetlock-joint to the ground. In such a case the obliquity of the long pastern will be the same as that of the toe (see Foot-Axis, p. 70).

Raising the toe by means of a tip, a full shoe with thinned branches or a toe-calk, *or paring away the quarters* will tilt the os pedis backward, break the foot-axis backward in the pedal joint and to a less extent in the coronary joint, and increase the tension of the perforans tendon considerably and of the perforatus slightly. These tendons tightening behind the fetlock-joint force it forward, causing the long pastern to stand steeper, and taking some strain from the suspensory ligament.

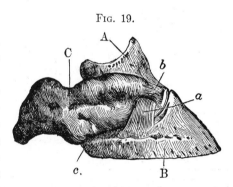

FIG. 19.

Right forefoot viewed from the external side: *A*, os coronæ; *B*, os pedis; *C*, external lateral cartilage; *a*, lateral pedal ligament; *b*, ligament uniting the lateral cartilage with the os coronæ; *c*, aponeurosis joining lateral cartilage and os pedis.

Hence, *the perforans tendon is under greatest tension, and the suspensory ligament under least tension, when the foot-axis is broken strongly backward.*

Shortening the toe, or raising the quarters by heel-calks or thickened branches, will tilt the os pedis forward, break the foot-axis forward in the pedal joint, and will *greatly lessen the tension of the perforans tendon.* The aggregate tension of perforans and perforatus tendons being diminished, the fetlock sinks downward and backward, the long pastern assumes a more nearly horizontal direction, and the tension of the suspensory ligament is increased. Thus, *the perforans tendon is under least tension, and the suspensory ligament under greatest strain, when the foot-axis is broken strongly forward.*

D. The Elastic Parts of the Foot.

All bodies which under pressure or traction change their form, but return again to their original shape as soon as the pressure or traction ceases, are called *elastic* or *springy.* Nearly

FIG. 20.

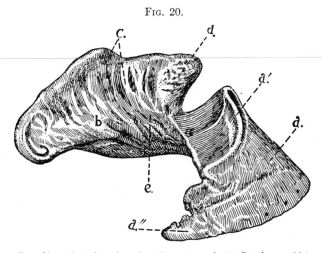

Os pedis and inner face of one lateral cartilage; *a*, toe of os pedis; *a'*, pyramidal eminence to which the extensor tendon attaches; *a''*, wing of pedal bone; *b*, lateral cartilage; *C*, points of attachment of suspensory ligament of lateral cartilage; *d*, point of insertion of ligament to the short pastern; *e*, point of insertion of ligaments from navicular bone.

all parts of the horse's foot, except the bones, possess more or less elasticity. The *lateral cartilages* and the *plantar cushion* are elastic to a high degree, but the *coronary band,* the *laminæ,* the *articular cartilage,* and the horny box or *hoof* are less elastic. This property or characteristic is possessed by the respective parts of the foot in accordance with their function, location, and structure.

The **two lateral cartilages** (Figs. 19, *C* and 20, *b*) are

FIG. 21.

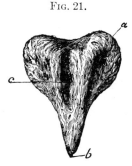

Plantar cushion seen from below: *a*, base or bulb of the plantar cushion; *b*, summit; *c*, median lacuna or cleft in which lies the "frog-stay" of the horny frog.

FIG. 22.

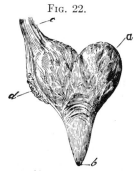

Plantar cushion seen from above: *a*, base (bulbs) of same; *b*, summit; *c*, supensory ligament of plantar cushion; *d*, place at which the elastic ligament connecting the os suffraginis and the lateral cartilage unites with the plantar cushion.

irregular, quadrangular plates, attached to the wings of the os pedis, and extending so far upward and backward that one can feel them yield to pressure on the skin above the coronet, and can thus test their elasticity. The perforans tendon and the plantar cushion lie between the lateral cartilages, and on the sides and behind are partially enclosed by them. The internal concave surface of the lateral cartilage (Fig. 20) is attached to the p l a n t a r

FIG. 23.

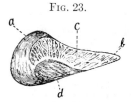

Section lengthwise through middle of the plantar cushion: *a*, glome (bulb) of heels; *b*, apex or point of fleshy frog; *c*, fibro fatty tissue of plantar cushion; *d*, median cleft which receives the frog-stay of the horny frog.

cushion, the os pedis, and the navicular bone, and, like the external, slightly convex surface, is covered with many blood-vessels (veins) Fig. 25, *B*).

The **plantar cushion** (Figs. 21, 22, 23) is composed almost entirely of yellow elastic and white fibrous tissues, with adipose (fat) cells distributed throughout their substance. It is similar in form to the horny frog, and lies between it and the perforans tendon (Fig. 24, *a*). The bulbs are formed by the posterior thicker portion which lies between the lateral cartilages and is divided into two parts by the cleft or median lacuna (Figs. 21, *a, a*nd 23, *d*). The summit is attached to the plantar face of the os pedis in front of the semilunar crest, and the bulbs are attached to the lateral cartilages. It is covered inferiorly by the velvety tissue of the frog (pododerm).

FIG. 24.

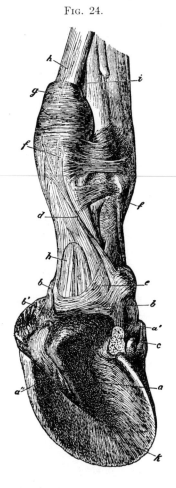

Right forefoot viewed from below, behind, and the external side. This figure shows clearly the position of the plantar cushion. The external lateral cartilage and the tissues covering the plantar cushion and under surface of the os pedis (velvety tissue of the sole and fleshy frog) have been removed: *a*, fleshy frog or plantar cushion; *a'*, bulbs of plantar cushion; the remaining visible parts belong to the so-called "fleshy frog;" *a''*, groove (median lacuna) in the lower surface of the fleshy frog, in which lies the frog-stay of the horny frog; *b*, suspensory ligament of the plantar cushion passing out of the bulbs; *b'*, small elastic cords passing to the lateral cartilage; *c*, elastic ligament coming from the lateral cartilage and uniting with the suspensory ligament of the plantar cushion; *d*, small tendinous cord beginning in the skin behind the fetlock-joint and ending on the os suffraginis in common with *b* and *c*; *e*, tendinous reinforcing sheath of the perforans tendon; *f*, reinforcing stay of the perforatus tendon; *g*, perforatus tendon; *h*, perforans tendon; *i*, suspensory ligament of the fetlock; *k*, plantar surface of the os pedis, to which the plantar cushion is joined by fibrous bands.

E. The Blood-Vessels and Nerves.

Vessels which carry blood from the heart to the tissues are called **arteries,** while those which return the blood to the heart from the tissues are called **veins.** Arteries and veins are connected by very small, thread-like vessels called *capillaries,* which originate in the smallest arteries and are so minute that they can not be seen without the aid of a microscope. The capillaries penetrate the soft tissues in every direction, and finally unite to form small veins. For our purpose we need consider only the arteries and veins.

The **arteries** carrying blood from the heart ramify and subdivide in all parts of the body, and thus reach the foot. They are thick-walled, very elastic tubes, **without valves,** and carry **bright-red** blood, which flows in spurts, as can be seen when an artery is cut. If a finger be pressed lightly over an artery lying near the surface, the blood-wave can be felt as a light stroke (pulse). The character of the pulse is important, because in inflammations of the pododerm or horn-producing membrane of the foot we can ascertain by feeling that the pulse is stronger than usual in the large arteries carrying blood to the inflamed foot.

On either side of the phalanges below the fetlock-joint there lies an artery called the *digital artery* (Fig. 25, *a*). The pulse can be felt in it as it passes over the fetlock at *A,* Fig. 25. It gives off the following collateral (side) branches: 1. The *artery of the first phalanx* (perpendicular artery), with anterior and posterior branches. 2. The *artery of the plantar cushion,* which supplies with blood the plantar cushion, the velvety tissue of the sole and frog, the bar portion of the coronary band, and the sensitive laminæ of the bars. 3. The *coronary artery,* which carries blood to the coronary band, os coronæ, ligaments of the coronary and pedal joints, flexor tendons, and skin.

The terminal branches of the digital arteries are the *preplantar* and *plantar ungual arteries.* The preplantar artery passes through the notch in the wing of the os pedis, then along the preplantar fissure, splitting up into many branches, which spread over and penetrate the porous surface of the os pedis. The

FIG. 25.

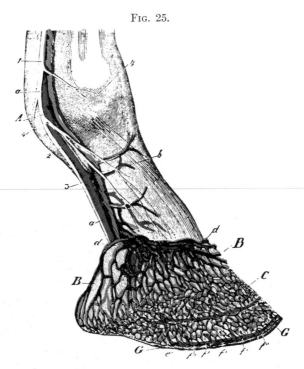

Side view of forefoot, showing blood-vessels and nerves: *a*, digital artery; *b*, anterior artery of the os suffraginis; *d*, anterior coronary artery, or circumflex artery of the coronet; *e,'* preplantar ungual artery; *f'*, inferior communicating arteries passing out from the semilunar artery of the os pedis, through minute holes just above the lower border of the bone; they unite to form (*f''*) the circumflex artery of the toe; *A*, digital vein; *B*, superficial venous plexus of coronary band and lateral cartilage; *C*, podophyllous venous plexus; *G*, circumflex vein of the toe; 1, plantar nerve; 2, anterior digital branch of same; 3, posterior digital branch of same; 4, small cutaneous branches of same.

plantar artery courses along the plantar fissure, enters the plantar foramen, and passes into the semilunar sinus of the os pedis, where it unites with the terminal branch of the opposite digital artery, forming the *semi-lunar arch.*

After the arterial or pure blood passes through the capillaries it is collected by the **veins,** to be returned to the heart; then it is driven to the lungs for purification, and is again returned to the heart, from whence it is pumped through the arteries to all parts of the body.

The veins are m o r e numerous than the arteries; they have thinner walls, and the larger ones are provided with **valves** that prevent the impure blood from flowing backward. T h e veins carry impure or **dark-red** blood towards the heart, and if one is opened the dark blood flows in a steady stream; it does not spurt. The great number of veinlets in the lower parts of the foot form a complex net-work (plexus) of vessels which are in such manifold· and close union with one another that checking the flow of blood in one part does not seriously interfere with the flowing of the blood towards the larger veins. The following are the most important of these

FIG. 26.

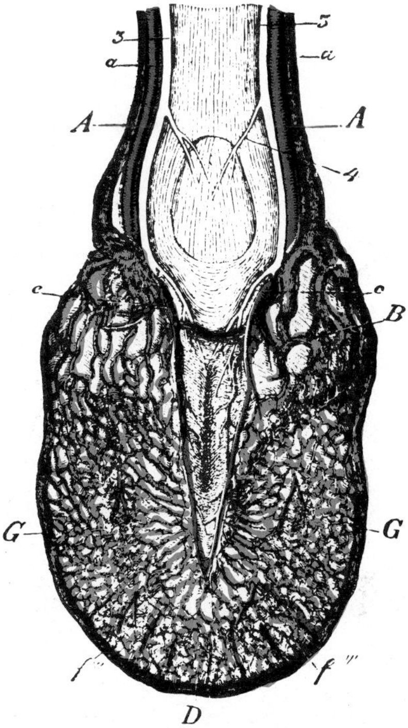

Foot viewed from below and behind: *a,* **digital** arteries; *c,* arteries of the plantar cushion; *f''',* small branches of the semilunar artery of the os pedis, which ramify in the velvety tissue of the sole; *A,* digital vein; *B,* venous plexus of the heels or bulbs; *D,* solar venous plexus; *G,* circumflex vein of the toe; 3, posterior digital branch of the plantar nerve; 4, cutaneous branches of the same.

net-works of veins or venous plexuses: (1) the *solar venous plexus* (Fig. 26, *D*); (2) the *podophyllous venous plexus* (Fig. 25, *C*); (3) *superficial coronary venous plexus* (Fig. 25, *B*);

(4) *bulbar venous plexus* (Fig. 26, *B*). All these plexuses of small veins contribute to form the *digital veins* (Figs. 25 and 26, *A*).

Nerves are roundish white cords which come from the brain and spinal cord; they generally accompany arteries. They divide and subdivide into smaller and smaller branches till they become invisible to the naked eye and are lost in the tissues. The nerves that are found in the foot come from the spinal cord, and because the largest nerves of the foot accompany the digital arteries they are called *digital nerves* (Fig. 25, 1). The branches ramify throughout all parts of the foot except the horny box and the hair. Nerves, according to their use or function, are classed as *motor* and *sensory*. The motor nerves end in muscles which they stimulate to action and control. The sensory nerves terminate in the skin and in the soft tissues just under the horny box or hoof (pododerm), and render these parts sensitive; that is, they convey certain feelings, as, for example, the pain caused by bruising, pricking, or close-nailing, to the brain and consciousness.

F. The Protective Organs of the Foot.

The protective organs are the skin and the horny box or hoof.

The *external skin,* or *hide,* covers the entire body; in the feet it covers the bones, tendons, and ligaments, even passing in under the hoof and directly covering the os pedis. This portion of the skin, enclosed by the hoof and therefore invisible, is called the *pododerm* or foot-skin. In Germany it is called the *hoof-skin* (huflederhaut), because it is a continuation of the outer visible skin, and because it secretes the hoof,—that is, the hoof is produced by it. That part of the skin which is covered with hair is known as the external or *hair-skin*.

(*a*) **The hair-skin** (Fig. 27, *a*) consists of *three* superposed *layers,*—(1) the *external* superficial layer, or *epidermis;* (2) the *middle* layer, *derm* or leather-skin (so-called because leather is made from it); (3) the *internal* layer, or *subcutaneous connective tissue.*

1. The *external layer,* or *epidermis,* is composed merely of single flattened, horn-like cells (scales) lying side by side and over one another, and uniting to form one entire structure,—a thin, horn-like layer, without blood-vessels or nerves. It extends over the entire surface of the body, and protects the underlying, very sensitive middle layer from external influences. The oldest cell-layers lie on the outer surface, and are being continuously brushed off in patches or scales, while new ones are constantly being formed on the outer surface of the middle layer.

FIG. 27.

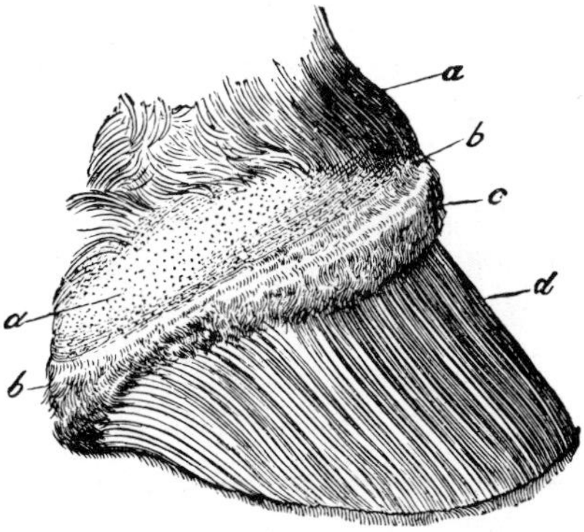

2. The *middle layer, leather-skin* or *dermis,* is composed of solid, fibrous, and elastic tissues, and contains many blood-vessels, small nerves, sweat- and oil-glands, and hair follicles from which the hair grows. The hair upon the posterior surface of the fetlock-joint is usually long and coarse, forming a tuft known as the "footlock," which encloses a horny spur, called the ergot. Common bred horses have, as a rule, larger and coarser footlocks than thoroughbreds.

Foot from which the horny capsule or hoof, has been removed by prolonged soaking: *a,* skin; on the left the hair has been rubbed away; *b,* perioplic band; *c,* coronary cushion; *d,* podophyllous tissue (fleshy leaves); at the lower border of the figure can be seen the minute thread-like processes or villi which grow down from the lower end of each fleshy leaf.

The derm or leather-skin, which produces the hair and epiderm, is the thickest and most important layer of the skin.

3. *The inner layer, or subcutaneous tissue,* unites the middle layer with the muscles, tendons, ligaments, bones, or other structures. It is that loose fibrous mesh or net-work through which the butcher cuts in removing the hide from the carcass.

(*b*) **The hoof-skin** (Figs. 27 and 28, *b, c, d*), or pododerm, is completely enclosed by the hoof. Although it is only an extension of the derm or middle layer of the hair-skin, it differs from the latter in structure and relations.

In order to study the pododerm we should not wrench the hoof off with violence, but should allow the foot to partially decompose by leaving it for six to eight days at ordinary room temperature; it can then be removed without injuring the pododerm. After the hoof has been removed the entire pododerm presents a more or less dark-red color (flesh-color), which is due to the great number of blood-vessels that it contains. For this reason different parts of the pododerm have received the prefix " fleshy," as for example, fleshy wall, fleshy sole, fleshy frog, etc. The pododerm is what the uninformed horseshoer calls the " quick." I will here remark that the three layers of the external or hair-skin are represented in the foot; however, the

Fig. 28.

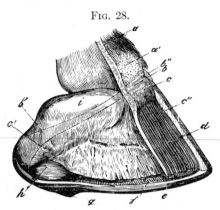

Foot from which the near half of the horny wall and a greater part of the so-called fleshy wall have been removed, in order to show the relation of the lateral cartilage to adjacent structures: *a*, vertical section of the skin prolonged downward through the pododerm (foot-skin) to show clearly that the latter is but a continuation of the former; *a'*, hairless place on the skin; *b*, perioplic band; *b'*, line indicating the upper border of the same; *b''*, surface of section of the periople, or perioplic horn-band; *c*, coronary cushion; *c'*, (left) line which marks the upper border of the coronary cushion; *c''*, section of wall at the toe; *d*, podophyllous tissue (sensitive laminæ); *e*, horny sole; *f*, white line; *g*, horny frog; *h*, fleshy frog; *i*, lateral cartilage.

epidermis is in an entirely different form,—namely, the horny box or hoof. The internal layer or subcutaneous tissue of the hair-skin is absent in those parts of the foot where the pododerm covers the os pedis. There remains, therefore, only the middle layer, derm, or *pododerm, which secretes the hoof,* and which is the prolongation and representative of the middle layer of the hair-skin. The pododerm is distinguished from the derm of the hair-skin chiefly by the absence of hairs, oil- and sweat-glands, and the presence on its outer surface of fleshy, sensitive laminæ and small thread-like projections called villi.

The pododerm consists of five different parts: the *perioplic band,* the *coronary band,* the *sensitive laminæ* (podophyllous tissue), the *velvety tissue of the sole,* and the *velvety tissue of the fleshy frog.*

1. *The perioplic band* (Fig. 28, *b*) is a narrow ridge, about one-fifth to one-fourth of an inch wide, lying between the hair-skin and the coronary band. Somewhat broader at the toe than on the sides, it broadens out near the bulbs of the heels, over which it passes to end in the velvety tissue of the fleshy frog. It is separated from the coronary band by a narrow depression called the *coronary furrow* (Moeller). The surface of the perioplic band glistens faintly, and is thickly studded with numerous thread-like projections called villi, which are from one-twenty-fourth to one-twelfth of an inch in length. **The perioplic band secretes the soft horn of the perioplic ring and the perioplic or varnish-like outer layer of the wall.**

2. *The coronary band* (Fig. 27, *c*) lies between the perioplic band and the sensitive laminæ or fleshy leaves. It presents a prominent convex band or cushion about three-fourths of an inch wide, which extends entirely around the foot from one bulb of the heel to the other. In front it directly covers the anterior extensor tendon of the toe, and at the sides the lateral surfaces of the os coronæ and the upper part of the lateral cartilages, while farther back towards the heels the lateral cartilages project considerably above both coronary and perioplic bands. The coronary band is more convex (rounded) in front than on the sides of the foot, and is flattened in the region of the bulbs of the heels. Its surface is thickly covered with villi, which are longer and stronger than those of the perioplic band. At the bulbs of the heels the coronary band turns forward and inward along the fleshy frog nearly to its summit. This portion of the coronary band is from one-third to one-half an inch wide,

and is called the *bar portion of the coronary band*. It is also covered with villi, which are directly continuous with those of the fleshy frog. **The coronary band secretes the principal part (middle layer) of the horny wall of the hoof, including the bar portion (bars) of the wall.**

3. *The fleshy wall,* or *podophyllous tissue* (Figs. 27, 28, *d,* and 29, *a*), is all that portion of the pododerm on which there are fleshy leaves. This leafy tissue covers the anterior surface

FIG. 29.

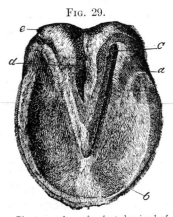

Plantar surface of a foot deprived of its horny capsule by prolonged maceration: *a*, laminæ of the bars; *b*, velvety tissue of the sole; *c*, velvety tissue of the frog; *d*, median cleft of the fleshy frog, into which the velvety tissue dips; *e* bulbar portion of the perioplic band, which passes insensibly into the velvety tissue of the fleshy frog.

of the os pedis and the lower portion of the external surface of the lateral cartilages. At the bulbs of the heels it turns inward at a sharp angle and extends forward and inward, between the bar portion of the coronary band and the posterior part of the velvety tissue of the sole, nearly to the middle of the solar surface of the foot, to form the *laminæ of the bars* (Fig. 29, *a*). The fleshy wall and fleshy bars are not covered with villi, but with numerous prominent, parallel, *fleshy leaves* placed close together, each of which runs in a straight line downward and forward from the coronary band to the lower border of the os pedis.

Between the fleshy leaves are deep furrows in which, in a foot which has not been deprived of its horny capsule, lie the horny or insensitive leaves of the wall. The fleshy leaves (podophyllous laminæ) are related to one another somewhat as the leaves of a book; their posterior borders are attached to the body or basement membrane of the fleshy wall, while their anterior borders and sides are free. At their upper ends immediately below the coronary band the leaves are quite narrow, but they gradually increase in width down to the middle, and thereafter maintain that breadth to the lower border of the os pedis, where they terminate in free, fleshy villi, which differ in no respect from those of the fleshy sole. The number and length of the fleshy leaves vary; in a medium-sized foot there are about five hundred, while in a large foot there may be as many as six hundred. On the anterior surface of the os pedis the leaves are thickest and longest; on the sides and quarters they gradually decrease in length, while in the bar region they are the shortest and gradually disappear near the anterior ends of the bars. The width of the leaves decreases as they become shorter. Viewed with the naked eye the leaves appear flat and smooth, but under the microscope one can see on both sides of a fleshy leaf numerous small, fleshy leaflets parallel to one another and extending lengthwise with the larger leaf. The large ones are called *principal leaves,* and the small ones are known as *collateral leaves,* or simply as *leaflets.*

The fleshy leaves (podophyllous tissue) secrete the horny leaves (keraphyllous tissue) and serve to bind the horny wall to the pododerm. The strength of this union is due largely to the dovetailing of the horny leaves and their leaflets with the fleshy leaves and their leaflets.

4. *The fleshy sole* or *velvety tissue of the sole* (Fig. 29, *b*) is that part of the pododerm which covers all the under surface of the foot except the plantar cushion, the bar laminæ, and the bar portion of the coronary band. It is sometimes slate-colored or studded with black spots, but is usually dark red. It is thickly set with villi, which are especially long and strong * near its periphery. The fleshy sole covers the solar plexus, or net-work of veins, and secretes the horny sole.

5. *The velvety tissue of the frog* (Fig. 29, *c*) covers the

---

* In order to see the length, thickness, and abundance of the villi of the pododerm, place the foot deprived of its hoof in a clear glass jar and cover it with water, renewing the latter until it is no longer tinged with blood.

lower surface of the plantar cushion, and in the region of the bulbs (e) passes insensibly into the perioplic band. In comparison with the fleshy sole, it has much finer and shorter villi and contains fewer blood-vessels. **It secretes the soft, horny frog.**

(c) **The horn capsule or hoof** (Fig. 30) is the entire mass made up of the horn-cells secreted from the whole surface of the pododerm, and next to the shoe is the organ with which the horse-shoer has most to do. The horn capsule or hoof is nothing more than a very thick epidermis that protects the horse's foot, just as a well-fitting shoe protects the human foot. The hoof of a sound foot is so firmly united with the underlying pododerm that only an extraordinary force can separate them. In its normal condition the hoof exactly fits the soft structures within it; hence it is evident that local or

FIG. 30.

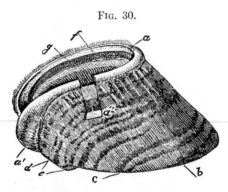

Side view of hoof recently removed: a, the perioplic horn-band; it is swollen from prolonged maceration in water; the upper border shows adhering hairs; the inner surface (perioplic groove) presents many minute openings; a', the perioplic horn-band broadens in passing over the bulb or glome of the heel, and is finally lost in the horny frog; a'', section of wall removed. That part of hoof on the right of b is called the toe; between b and c is the side wall or "mamma," and between c and d the "quarter;" e, projecting horny frog; f, coronary groove with numerous minute openings; g, keraphyllous layer of the wall (horny leaves).

general contraction of the hoof must produce pressure on the blood-vessels and nerve-endings of the pododerm, disturb the circulation of the blood and the nutrition of the foot, and cause pain.

The hoof is divided into three principal parts, which are solidly united in the healthy foot,—namely, the **wall,** the **sole,** and the **frog.** That part of the hoof which is almost wholly visible when the foot is on the ground (Fig. 30, b, c), and which protects the foot in front and upon the sides, is known as the **wall.** In position, course, direction, and arrangement of its parts it simulates the different parts of the pododerm from which it is developed. It extends from the edge of the hair just above the coronary band to the ground; backward it gradually decreases in height (length), passes around the bulbs of the heels, and turns forward and inward (Fig. 32, *d, e,* and 34, *a, b*) to form the **bars,** which are finally lost in the edge of the sole near the summit of the frog. It thus forms at each heel an angle (Fig. 31, *d,* and 32, *d*) known as a buttress, which encloses a branch of the horny sole. Externally the wall is smooth, covered with the varnish-like periople, and presents indistinct ring-like markings (Fig. 30). Its inner surface, on the contrary, presents a great n u m b e r of horn-leaves which are spoken of collectively as the *keraphyllous tissue* (Figs. 32, *g,*

FIG. 31.

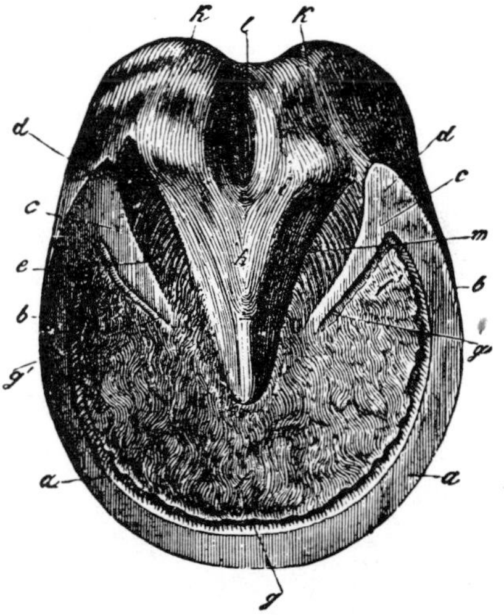

Plantar surface of right fore-hoof: *a, a,* bearing-surface of the toe; *a, b,* bearing-surface of the side walls or mammæ; *b c,* bearing-surface of the quarters; *d,* buttress, or angle formed by wall and bar; *e,* bar; *f,* sole; *f',* branches of the sole; *g,* white line; it passes between the sole and bars and ends at *g';* *h,* horny frog; *i,* branches of the frog; *k,* heels, bulbs, or glomes of the hoof; *l,* median lacuna of horny frog. Between the bars and the horny frog lie the lateral lacunæ of the frog.

and 35, *f*). The upper or **coronary border** of the wall is thin and flexible, and on its inner aspect is the **coronary groove,** into which fits the **coronary band** (Fig. 30, *f*). The lower border of the wall, called the " **bearing-edge** " or *plantar border* (Fig. 31, *a*), is the one to which the horseshoe is fastened. By dividing a hoof from before to behind along its median line, *outer* and *inner* halves or *walls* are produced, and by dividing the entire lower circumference of the wall into five equal parts or sections, a **toe,** two **side walls or mammæ,** and two **quarters** will be exhibited (Figs. 32 and 33). In order to designate these regions of the hoof still more accurately, they are spoken of as outer and inner toes, quarters, and heels.

The direction (slant) *and length of the wall* vary in one and the same hoof, as well as between fore and hind hoofs. The portion of the wall of fore hoofs is the most slanting,—that is, forms the most acute angle with the surface of the ground,—and is also the longest. Towards the quarters the wall gradually ,becomes very nearly vertical; in almost all hoofs the posterior part of the quarters slants downward and inward towards the median vertical antero-posterior plane of the foot. At the same time the wall, in passing back from the toe to the heel, becomes gradually shorter in such a manner that the heights of the toe, side walls, and quarters are related to one another about as 3 : 2 : 1 in front hoofs and as 4 : 3 : 2 in hind hoofs. The outer wall is, as a rule, somewhat more slanting than the inne·. Viewing a foot in profile, the toe and heel should be parallel; that is, the line from the hair to the ground at the toe should be parallel to the line from the hair to the ground at the buttress. **All deviations of the wall from a straight line** (out-

FIG. 32.

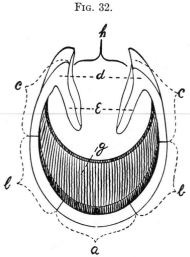

Wall and bars seen from below: *a*, toe; *b*, side-wall, or mamma; *c*, quarter; *d*, buttress; *e*, bar; *g*, horn leaves; *h*, space occupied by the frog.

ward or inward bendings) **are to be regarded as faults or defects.**

The *thickness of the wall* is also variable. In front hoofs the wall is thickest at the toe, and becomes gradually thinner towards the quarters, while in hind hoofs, there is very little difference in the thickness of the wall of the toe, sides, and quarters. *The more slanting half of the hoof is always the thicker;* thus, for example, the outer wall of a base-wide foot is always longer and more oblique than the inner wall,

FIG. 33.

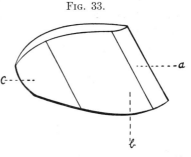

A hoof in profile; *a*, toe (one half); *b*, side wall; *c*, quarter.

and is also thicker. According to Mayer, the thickness of the wall at the toe varies from three- to five-eighths of an inch, and at the quarters from two to three eighths of an inch. These measurements are dependent upon the size and breeding of the horse.

The horn wall is composed of *three superposed l a y e r s.* These from without to within are: (1) the **periople,** secreted by the perioplic band. It is very t h i n ,

FIG. 34.

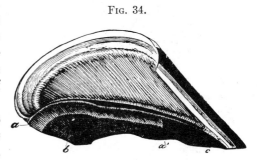

Vertical section through the middle of a hoof, with horny frog removed, to show the position of the bar: *a, b,* marks the line at which the wall bends forward and inward towards the median line of the foot to become the bar. Bar runs forward and passes imperceptibly into the sole *c; a, a',* the light shading shows the part of the bar that was in contact with the horny frog.

glistening, and varnish-like in appearance, and covers the entire outer surface of the wall, except where it has been removed by the rasp, and prevents rapid evaporation of moisture from the horn. (2) The middle or **protective layer** (Fig. 35, *d*) is the thickest, strongest, and most important of the three layers; it forms the principal mass of the wall, and is developed or secreted by the coronary band, which fits into the coronary groove. There are in the coronary groove a great number of small, funnel-shaped openings into which project the horn-producing villi or papillæ of the coro-

FIG. 35.

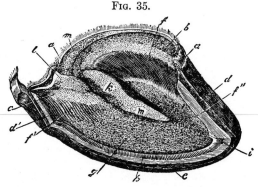

The outer wall of the hoof has been removed by cutting vertically through the middle of the toe, down to the upper surface of the sole, then horizontally backward into the quarter, and, finally, upward through the quarter: *a*, perioplic horn-band; *b*, coronary groove; it turns inward and forward at *c* to form the upper border of the bar; *d*, surface of section of the wall at the toe; *d'*, at the quarter; *e*, surface of horizontal section of the wall near its lower border; *f*, keraphyllous layer of the wall; at *f'* it turns forward and inward to cover the bar; *f''*, horny leaves standing free and passing insensibly into the white horn of the middle layer or true wall; *g*, horny sole; *h*, white line; *i*, small horn-spur in middle of toe; *k*, part of horny frog which is in intimate union with the upper edge of the bar; *l*, frog-stay of horny frog; it divides the trough-like depression of the upper surface of the frog into *m*, the two upper channels of the frog.

nary band. (3) The **inner layer or keraphyllous layer** (Fig. 35, *f*) consists of prominent, parallel horn-leaves lying side by side over the entire inner surface of the middle layer of the wall, and continuing beyond the buttresses to the ends of the bars (Fig. 35, *f'*). This layer of horn-leaves (keraphyllous layer) has in a general way about the same shape and arrangement as the layer of fleshy leaves (podophyllous layer) which secretes it; for the horn-leaves fit in with the fleshy leaves in such a way that every fleshy leaf is embraced by two horn-leaves, and every horn-leaf by two fleshy leaves (Fig. 36). The keraphyllous layer and the horn of the inmost part of the middle or protective layer are always white, even in pigmented (colored) hoofs.

The **horn sole** (Fig. 31, *f,* and Fig. 35, *g*) is secreted by the velvety tissue of the sole. A sole from which the loose

FIG. 36.

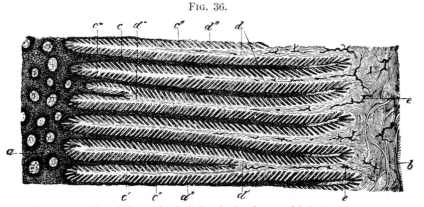

Cross-section of keraphyllous and podophyllous laminæ (horny and fleshy leaves): *a*, inmost part of the solid wall; the horn-tubes approach very close to the horny leaves; *b*, body of the podophyllous membrane; *c*, horny portion of a horn-leaf directly continuous with the middle or principal layer of the wall; *c'*, a rudimentary horn-leaf that does not reach the body of the podophyllous membrane; *c''*, cross-section of horny leaves from the sides of which branch many secondary leaves (leaflets) composed of soft (young) horn-cells. These soft cellular horn-leaflets dovetail with the podophyllous or fleshy leaflets; *d*, podophyllous laminæ extending from the body of the podophyllous membrane; *d'*, podophyllous laminæ which have branched in their course to the wall, and thus given rise to *c'*, rudimentary horn-leaves; *d''*, cross-section of podophyllous leaflets extending from the sides of the podophyllous leaves; each two such leaflets secrete a keraphyllous leaflet between them; *e*, injected arterial vessels.

flakes of old horn have been removed is about as thick as the wall. It covers the under surface of the foot, and presents upon its upper surface a convexity which exactly fits into the concavity on the under surface of the os pedis. This upper surface is thickly covered by a multitude of minute funnel-shaped openings for the reception of the villi of the velvety tissue of the sole (Fig. 37). The lower surface of the sole is more or less concave, rough, uneven, and often covered by loose scales of dead horn. Behind, the sole presents a triangular opening whose borders lie partly in contact with the horny frog and partly with the bars. This opening or re-entering angle divides the sole into a *body* (Fig. 31, *f*) and two wings or *branches* (Fig. 31, *f′*). The outer border of the sole unites through the medium of the **white line** with the lower part of the inner surface of the wall,—that is, with the keraphyllous

FIG. 37.   FIG. 38.

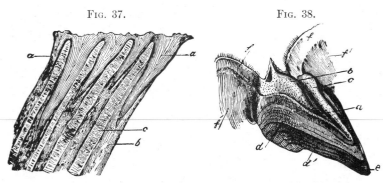

Vertical section of the horny sole magnified: *a*, funnel-shaped openings which contain the horn-producing villi of the fleshy sole; they are of various sizes; *b*, horn-tubes; *c*, intertubular horn.

Horny frog, with the posterior portion of the perioplic horn-band and the periople which covers the quarters removed from the hoof as one piece by maceration: *a*, trough-shaped depression of upper surface, which is divided posteriorly into the two upper channels of the frog by *b*, the frog-stay; *c*, part of the frog that is joined to the bar and forms the lateral wall of the depression (channels) on upper surface of frog; *d*, lateral surface of horny frog which, in its upper part, adheres to the bar, but below, at *d′*, lies free; *e*, point or summit of the frog; *f*, perioplic horn-band; *f′*, periople of the quarters.

layer of the wall. This **white line** (Figs. 31, *g*, and 35, *h*), of so much importance to the horseshoer, is formed by the horn-leaves, and by those short plugs of tubular horn which are secreted by the villi that are always found at the lower ends of the fleshy leaves. The white line may be said to exist wherever the horn-leaves can be discerned upon the plantar surface of the hoof. It not only passes around the circumference of the sole from heel to heel, but may be followed forward from the buttresses along the bars almost to the summit of the frog. The horn of the white line is soft, unpigmented (white), and possesses so very little resistance (strength) that it is often found crumbling or even absent in places. The visible part of the white line is usually of a grayish-black color, owing to the working in from below of dirt and liquid manure, and to staining by rust from the nails. **The white line is very important, since it serves as the point from which we judge of the thickness of the wall, and because the horseshoe nail should penetrate it.**

A horny frog cut vertically and lengthwise through its middle: *a*, upper surface; *b*, frog-stay; *c*, median lacuna of frog, which at *c'*, is overlaid with superposed layers of horn.

The Frog (Figs. 31, *h*, 35, *k*, *l*, 38 and 39), secreted by the velvety tissue covering the plantar cushion and presenting almost the same form as the latter, lies as a wedge between the bars and between

FIG. 40.

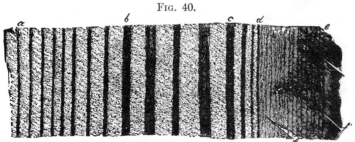

Longitudinal section of the wall magnified. The dark stripes parallel and close together are horn-tubes; the lighter surface between the tubes represents the intertubular horn. Notice that the horn-tubes are of various diameters. The space between *a* and *b* represents the small tubes of the outer, darker horn of the principal (middle) layer of the wall; the space between *b* and *c* the lighter, inner horn of the wall; *c*, *d*, the horn separating the wall proper from the horny leaves; *d*, *e*, the horny leaves (keraphyllous tissue), on which can be seen fine, parallel, vertical stripes; in the horn-leaf at *f*, *f'*, are seen fissures passing obliquely upward and outward towards the wall.

the edges of the sole just in front of the bars, with both of which structures it is intimately united. Its horn is *quite soft* and *very elastic*. The median lacuna or cleft of the frog (Fig. 31, *l*) divides it into two branches (Fig. 31, *i*), which pass backward and outward into the horny bulbs (Fig. 31, *k*). In front of the median lacuna the two branches unite to form the *body* of the frog (Fig. 31, *h*), which ends in a point, designated the *point,* apex, or summit of the frog. On the upper surface of the frog, directly over the median cleft of the lower surface, there is a small projection called the frog-stay (Figs. 35, *l,* 38 and 39, *b*), which fits into the median cleft of the plantar cushion. Besides, the upper surface of the frog shows many minute openings, similar to but smaller than those of the sole and coronary groove, for the reception of villi. In unshod hoofs the frog, sole, bars, and bearing-edge of the wall are on a level; that is, the plantar surface of such hoofs is perfectly flat.

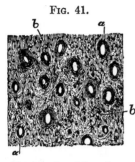

FIG. 41.

b   *a*

b

a

Cross-section of the wall, magnified: *a,* horn-tubes; *b,* intertubular horn.

The *minute structure of the horn* can scarcely be considered in detail in an elementary treatise such as this is. However, a few of the most important facts are as follows:

If we carefully examine a transverse section of the horn of the wall (Fig. 41), sole, or frog, we will see with the naked eye, though much better with a magnifying glass, many minute points quite close to one another, and greatly resembling the small openings which we have seen in the coronary groove of the wall and on the upper surface of the horny sole and frog. If, now, we examine a longitudinal section of the wall (Fig. 40) or sole, we will see a number of fine, dark stripes which are straight, parallel, quite close to one another, of different widths, and which are separated by bands of lighter horn also of different widths. A thin section or slice of the wall taken at right angles to the direction of these dark lines (Fig. 41) shows us that the minute points that are visible to the naked eye, when held up to the light or moderately magnified, prove to be small openings (Fig. 41, *a*). Since these openings, shown in Fig. 41, represent the dark lines shown in Fig. 40, because an opening is found wherever there is a dark line, *we must regard all dark lines seen in longitudinal sections of wall, sole, and frog as hollow cylinders or tubes,* though they are not always hollow, but are often filled with loosely adjusted, crumbling, broken-down horn-cells. The dark edges of the openings (*a*) consist of thick layers of horn-cells (tube-walls). The entire structure is called a **horn-tube,** and the lighter-colored masses of horn (Fig. 41, *b*) between the tubes are known as **intertubular horn.**

With the exception of the horny leaves of the wall and bars, all the horn of the hoof is composed of horn-tubes and intertubular horn.

The horn-tubes of the wall, sole, and frog always run downward and forward parallel to the direction of the wall at the toe,—that is, in a direction parallel with the inclination of the hoof as a whole. Although the wall, sole, and frog differ from one another considerably with respect to the size and number of the horn-tubes, the quality of the intertubular horn, and the thickness and strength of the horn-cells, these differences are only of subordinate interest or importance to the horseshoer; but he who desires to learn more of this matter is referred to the work of Leisering & Hartmann, " Der Fuss des Pferdes in Rücksicht auf Bau, Verrichtungen und Hufbeschlag," eighth edition, Dresden, 1893. This book also treats of the variations in the quality of hoofs, which is very important for the practical horseshoer to know. It, furthermore, considers the solidity and strength of the horn of the different parts of the hoof.

With respect to solidity, two kinds of horn are distinguished, —namely, **hard** and **soft horn.** The periople, the white line, and the frog are soft horn structures; the middle layer of the wall and the sole are hard or solid horn. The wall, however, is somewhat harder and more tenacious than the sole, for the latter passes off in more or less large flakes (exfoliates) or crumbles away on its lower surface, at least in shod feet, while no such spontaneous shortening occurs in the wall.

Soft horn differs from hard horn in that its horn-cells never become hard and horn-like. It is very elastic, absorbs water quickly, and as readily dries out and becomes very hard and

Fig. 42.

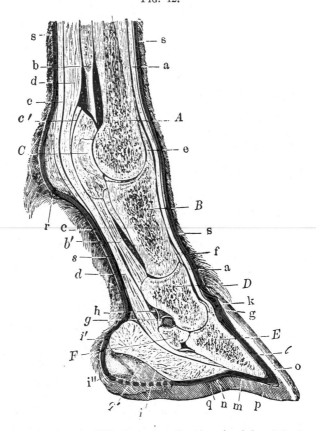

Vertical section through middle of a forefoot, the skin and pododerm being in red. (In the figure the direction of both long and short pasterns, *B* and *D*, is too nearly vertical—too steep). *A*, metacarpal bone (cannon); *B*, os suffraginis (long pastern); *C*, inner sesamoid bone (to render it visible a portion of the intersesamoid ligament was removed); *D*, os coronæ (short pastern); *E*, os pedis (foot-bone); *F*, navicular bone; *a*, extensor tendon; *b*, suspensory ligament of the fetlock; *b'*, superficial inferior sesamoid ligament; *c*, perforatus tendon or flexor of the os coronæ; *c'*, ring passing forward from this tendon and encircling the perforans tendon; *d*, perforans tendon; *e*, capsular ligament of fetlock-joint; *f*, capsular ligament of coronary joint; *g*, *g'*, capsular ligament of pedal joint; *h*, synovial sheath of the perforans tendon; *i*, plantar cushion and fleshy frog; *i'*, bulbs or glomes of plantar cushion; *i''* indicates the lowest point reached by the plantar cushion, which in the figure is hidden below by the frog-stay of the horny frog; *k*, coronary band (red); *l*, podophyllous tissue (red); *m*, velvety tissue of the sole (red); *n*, velvety tissue of fleshy frog (red); *o*, wall; *p*, sole; *q*, frog; *q''*, the inner half of the frog-stay which reposes in the median lacuna of the fleshy frog; *s*, hair-skin (red).

brittle and easily fissured and chapped. With respect to *quality,* we distinguish good and bad horn; the former is fine and tenacious (tough), the latter coarse and either soft and crumbling or hard and brittle. If not dried out, all horn is elastic,

FIG. 43.

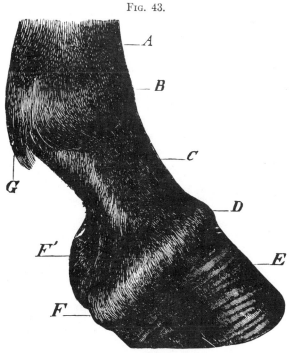

Right forefoot viewed from the side: *A,* lower end of the cannon; *B,* fetlock-joint; *C,* long pastern; *D,* coronet; *E,* hoof; *F,* heel; *F',* inner heel; *G,* foot-lock covering the ergot.

though soft horn is more elastic than hard. All horn is a *poor conductor of heat.*

The relative positions of the various parts of the foot are shown in Fig. 42.

Fig. 43 represents the exterior of a well-formed foot.

CHAPTER II.

THE FOOT IN ITS RELATION TO THE ENTIRE LIMB.

As there are well-formed and badly formed bodies, so there are well-formed and badly formed limbs and hoofs. The form of the hoof depends upon the position of the limb. A straight limb of normal direction possesses, as a rule, a regular hoof, while an oblique or crooked limb is accompanied by an irregular or oblique hoof. Hence, it is necessary, before discussing the various forms of the hoof, to consider briefly the various positions that may be assumed by the limbs. In this discussion we shall deal with the **living** horse.

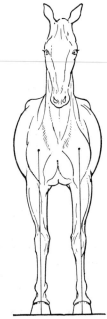

FIG. 44.

Normal (regular) position of fore-limbs.

A. Standing Positions of the Limbs.

The position of a limb depends upon the varying lengths of its component bones and the angles at which they meet one another. To judge the standing position of a fore-limb one must stand *in front* of the horse; to judge a hind limb, stand *behind* the horse; the backward or forward deviations of both front and hind limbs are judged by standing at the side. But a horse does not always move as his standing position would lead one to suspect; standing and moving are different. Therefore, in order to arrive at a proper judgment, one must observe the limbs both at rest and in motion.

(*a*) **The position of a limb viewed from in front is normal**

62

or straight (Fig. 44) when it stands vertical or perpendicular. A plumb-line dropped from the point of the shoulder (middle of the scapulo-humeral articulation) should pass down the middle line of the limb, dividing it into inner and outer halves of equal width, and meeting the ground at the middle of the toe.

In the *base-wide standing position* (Fig. 45) the plumb-line falls to the inner side of the limb; the limb extends obliquely downward and outward. To this class belong also the *knee-*

FIG. 45.   FIG. 46.   FIG. 47.

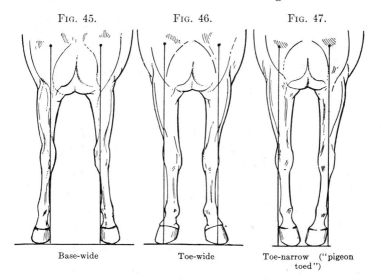

Base-wide   Toe-wide   Toe-narrow ("pigeon toed")

narrow (knock-kneed) *position,* in which the knees are too close together, while the feet stand wide apart, and the *toe-wide position* (splay-footed, Fig. 46) in which the toes point obliquely forward and outward. In base-wide positions either the entire limb extends downward and outward or the foot alone is turned outward.

The *base narrow position* is frequently observed in horses with very wide breasts. The limbs run downward and inward, a plumb-line dropped from the point of the shoulder falling to the outer side of the leg and foot. A special form of the base-narrow position is the *toe-narrow* or *pigeon-toed position* (Fig. 47). In some instances the legs are straight and perpendicular down to the fetlock, while from there to the ground the phalanges incline obliquely inward. Another form is the *knee-wide* or *bandy-legged position*, in which the knees are placed too far

FIG. 48.   FIG. 49.

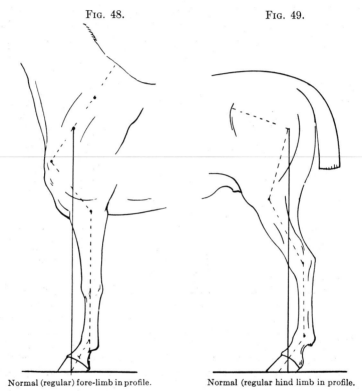

Normal (regular) fore-limb in profile.   Normal (regular hind limb in profile.

apart, while the cannons and phalanges incline downward and inward.

The position of a fore-limb viewed in profile is regular or normal (Fig. 48) when a perpendicular line dropped from the tuberosity of the acromian spine (point of union of the upper and middle thirds of the scapula or shoulder blade) divides the leg from the elbow to the fetlock into anterior and posterior halves of equal width, and touches the ground immediately back of the bulbs of the heel. A perpendicular line

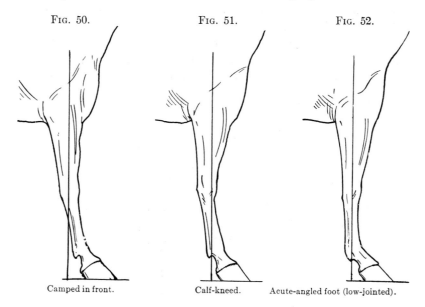

FIG. 50. FIG. 51. FIG. 52.

Camped in front. Calf-kneed. Acute-angled foot (low-jointed).

dropped from the point of union of the middle and lower thirds of the scapula (shoulder blade) will cut the humerus into halves, and meet the ground between the toe and the heel.*

---

* **In station of rest,** the normal position of a fore-leg, as seen from the side, is somewhat different. The *station of rest* is the position that is maintained with the least possible muscular effort. With gradual muscular relaxation the head and neck sink to a point somewhat below the line of the back, the top of the shoulder blade sinks a little, and the shoulder and elbow joints move forward till the centre of the elbow joint is directly above the ground-surface of the hoof. Therefore, when a horse *at rest* stands firmly on all four feet, *the fore-leg* viewed from the side, *has a normal* (regular) *direction, when a perpendicular line dropped from the tuberosity of the acromian spine passes through the middle of the elbow joint and meets the ground near the middle of the hoof.*

The *foot-axis* (line of direction of the three phalanges) and the wall at the toe form an angle of from forty-five to fifty degrees with the horizontal ground-surface.

From this normal or regular standing position, there are *deviations forward* as well as *backward*.

Forward Deviations.—*" Standing in front "* or *" camped in front "* (Fig. 50) is that position in which the entire leg from the body to the ground is placed too far forward. *Sheep-*

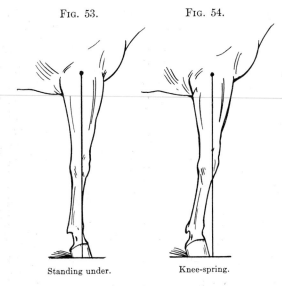

FIG. 53.   FIG. 54.

Standing under.   Knee-spring.

kneed (Fig. 51) is that position in which the forward deviation is from the knee downward, the knee being placed too far under the body. *" Weak-jointed," " low-jointed,"* or *" acute-angled "* (Fig. 52) is that position in which the limbs are perpendicular and straight down as far as the fetlock-joint, but the feet are placed too far in front.

Backward Deviations.—*Standing under in front* (Fig. 53) is that deviation in which the entire leg from the elbow down is placed back of the perpendicular line and, therefore, too far under the body. When this deviation affects only the cannon bone, the horse stands bent forward at the knees,—a condition known as *"goat-kneed," "buck-kneed," "over in the knees,"* or, more commonly, *"knee-sprung"* (Fig. 54). When the backward deviation is only from the fetlock down, the animal is said to stand *upright* or *"straight in the fetlock"* (Fig. 53).

(*b*) A hind leg viewed from behind is said to be *regular* or *straight* (Fig. 55) when a perpendicular line dropped from

FIG. 55.

FIG. 56.   FIG. 57.

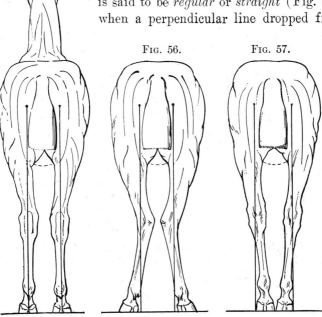

Normal (regular) position   Base-wide (cow hocked).   Base-narrow.
viewed from behind.

the tuberosity of the ischium (see Fig. 1, 9") divides the entire limb into inner and outer halves of equal width and touches the ground opposite the median lacuna of the frog. **Seen from the side,** this line just touches the point of the hock and, passing down at some distance from the flexor tendons, meets the ground considerably back of the heels. A perpendicular line dropped from the hip-joint should pass through the foot, meeting the ground half-way between the point of the toe and the heel (Fig. 49). There are base-wide, base-narrow, toe-wide, and toe-narrow deviations in the hind limbs as in the fore-limbs.

The hind limbs are *base-wide* when they, either as a whole or in part, deviate outward from the normal. The "*cow-hocked*" position (Fig. 56) is an example of the base-wide; in this case the points of the hocks are too close and turn towards each other, while the feet are widely separated and the toes turned outward. *Base-narrow* is that position of the hind legs in which either the entire leg deviates to the inner side of the perpendicular (Fig. 57), or the leg is about perpendicular down as far as the hock, but below this joint runs downward and inward (Fig. 58). In this latter case the hocks may be too far apart, the leg is bent outward at the hock and the animal is termed "*bandy-legged*," "*bow-legged*."

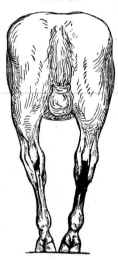

FIG. 58.

Base-narrow position of hind limbs (bandy-legged).

Viewing a hind limb from the side, it may be observed to deviate either forward or backward from the normal. Among forward deviations is the so-called "*sabre-leg*" or "*sickle-hock*" (Fig. 59), in which the hock-joint is too much flexed, the foot placed too far forward under the body, and the fetlock too slanting. In the position known as "*camped behind*" (Fig. 60) the leg is behind the body and the pastern is too upright, too nearly vertical.

It is possible for each limb of the same horse to assume a different direction. It more often happens that if the fore-limbs are base-wide the hind limbs are base-narrow, or *vice versa.* While there are some other deviations that differ somewhat from those already described, they are of less importance to the horseshoer.

B. Forms of Feet, Viewed from in Front, from Behind, and in Profile.

In all the various positions of the limbs we find the feet in one of the following *three forms,* or very closely approaching one of them. By means of a proper knowledge of these three forms,

Fig. 59.   Fig. 60.

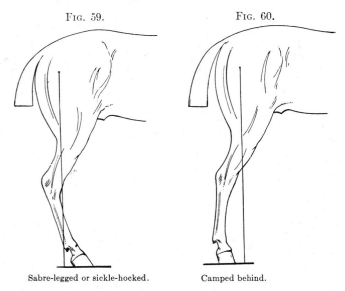

Sabre-legged or sickle-hocked.   Camped behind.

the judging of the form, flight of the foot in travelling, and preparation of the hoof for the shoe, as well as the choice of the length of the shoe, are regulated, facilitated, and simplified.

Whether a horse's feet be observed from *in front* or from *behind,* their form corresponds to, or at least resembles, either that of the **regular** position (Figs. 61 and 62), the **base-wide** or toe-wide position (Figs. 63 and 64), or the **base-narrow** or toe-narrow position (Figs. 65 and 66).

By the *direction* of the **foot-axis**—that is, an imaginary
line passing through the long axis of the three phalangeal bones
(Figs. 61, 65, 67, 68 and 69)—we determine whether or not
the hoof and pastern stand in proper mutual relation.

FIG. 61.   FIG. 62.

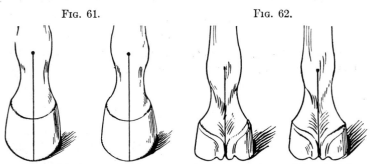

A pair of front feet of regular position viewed from in front and from behind.

In the regular standing position (Figs. 61 and 62) the
foot-axis runs straight downward and forward, in the base-

FIG. 63.   FIG. 64.

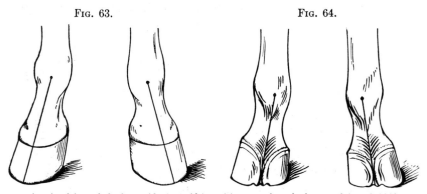

A pair of feet of the base-wide (toe-wide) position seen from in front and from behind.

wide position (Figs. 63 and 64) it runs obliquely downward
and outward, and in the base-narrow position (Figs. 65 and
66) it runs obliquely downward and inward.

Viewing the foot from the side, we distinguish the **regular** (normal) position (Fig. 68), and designate all forward deviations as **acute-angled** (long toe and low heel, Fig. 67), and

FIG. 65.   FIG. 66.

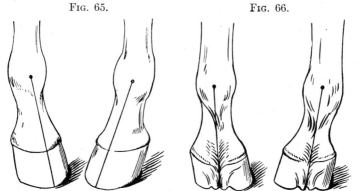

A pair of feet of the base-narrow (toe-narrow) position seen from in front and from behind.

all deviations backward from the regular position as **upright** (short toe and high heel, Fig. 69), steep-toed, or stumpy.

When the body-weight is uniformly distributed over all four

FIG. 67.   FIG. 68.   FIG. 69.

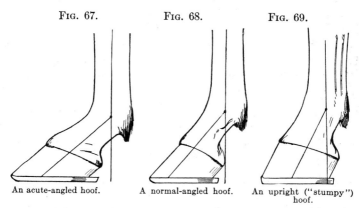

An acute-angled hoof.   A normal-angled hoof.   An upright ("stumpy") hoof.

limbs, the foot-axis should be *straight* (Figs. 67 and 69), not " broken " (bent) ; **the long pastern, wall at the toe, and foot-axis should have the same slant.**

A peculiar form of foot is the so-called *bear-foot* (Fig. 70), in which the foot-axis, viewed from the side, is broken strongly forward at the coronet. The wall at the toe stands much steeper than the long pastern and is more or less convex; in other words, a low-jointed, sloping pastern is attached to an upright hoof. Such a foot is sometimes improperly called a " club-foot."

C. Lines of Flight of Hoofs in Motion.

If we observe horses moving unrestrained over level ground, we will notice differences in the carriage of the feet. **Viewed from in front, or from behind,** in the *regular standing position* of the limbs the hoofs are carried forward in a *straight direction,*—that is, in a line parallel with the median line of the body (Fig. 71). The toes likewise point straight forward; the hoofs alight properly (flat) on the ground. If the horse stands *base-wide,* the hoof is carried in a circle; from its position, which is behind and well out from the median line, the hoof passes first forward and inward until it is close to the supporting leg, and then outward to the ground (Fig. 72), where the shock is received principally upon the outer toe. The toes point either directly forward, as in the regular standing position (Fig. 72), or forward and outward as in the toe-wide position (Fig. 73). In the toe-wide position the hoof in its flight may cross the median line.

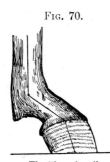

Fig. 70.

The "bear-foot."

Exactly the reverse is true of the horse that stands *base-narrow;* in this case the hoof is moved in a circle whose convexity is outward,—that is, the hoof from its position behind, and close to the median line, is carried forward and outward and then inward to the ground (Figs. 74 and 75).

Viewed from the side, the line of flight of a hoof is determined largely by the obliquity (slant) of the foot-axis.

1. With a straight foot axis of *normal slant* (45°–50°, Fig. 76, *A*), the hoof follows the arc of a circle and reaches its highest point when directly above the supporting hoof, *i.e.*, when half-way in the stride.

2. With a straight, but *acute-angled* foot-axis (less than 45°, Fig. 76, *B*), the hoof rises rapidly, reaches its highest

FIG. 71.   FIG. 72.   FIG. 73.   FIG. 74.   FIG. 75.

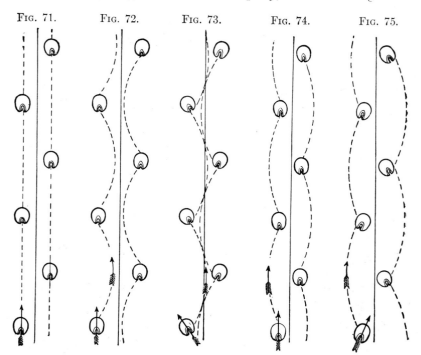

point before it has completed the first half of the stride, *i.e.*, before it has passed the supporting hoof, and descending gradually in a long curve alights easily on the ground.

3. With a straight, but upright foot-axis (55° or more, Fig. 76, *C*), the hoof rises slowly, reaches its highest point in front of the supporting hoof, from which point it descends rapidly. The gait is "choppy," and in the saddle horse un-

pleasant for the rider. *The length and the height of the stride are greatest in acute-angled feet; least in upright feet.* Furthermore, length and height of stride are in a measure dependent on breeding, training, condition of the legs (whether stiffened by use or disease), length of the hoof and the weight of the shoe.

Fig. 76.

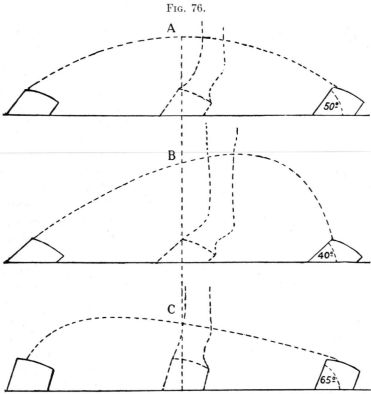

Flight of the hoof as seen from the side: *A*, flight of a regular hoof; *B*, flight of an acute-angled hoof; *C*, flight of an upright hoof.

Many deviations in the line of flight of hoofs and in the manner in which they are set to the ground occur; for example, horses heavily burdened or pulling heavy loads, and, therefore, not having free use of their limbs, project their limbs irregularly and meet the ground first with the toe; however, careful observation will detect the presence of one or the other of these lines of flight of the foot. Irregular carriage of the feet renders a horse unsuitable for general purposes only when it is very pronounced, in which case certain troublesome conditions, such as interfering and disease of joints, are of frequent occurrence.

D. The Influence of Weight in the Shoe or Otherwise Attached to the Hoof, in Altering the Flight of the Hoof.

There is nothing mysterious in the effect of weight upon the flight of the feet. On the contrary, the lines of flight are determined (as shown in pages 72–74, Figs. 71–76), *first,* by the relation of the transverse axes of the hinge-joints of the leg and foot to the line of progression (median line); *second,* by the length and obliquity of the hoof and pastern; *third,* by the height and length of stride which is natural to each individual.

Weight induces higher action and a longer stride. Inertia increases with the weight. A heavy shoe cannot be snatched from the ground as quickly as a light one, but when moving forward at a given velocity its greater momentum (momentum = mass (wt) $\times$ velocity : m = wt $\times$ v) carries the foot farther forward than does the lighter shoe. Thus, the heavier shoe, or weight attached to the hoof, lengthens the stride at both ends. The farther from the centre of rotation of the scapula the weight is placed, *i.e.,* the nearer to the toe it is placed, the greater the muscular effort required to start it and to stop it.

Height of action, though largely the result of breeding, temperament, and the exhilaration that accompanies perfect health and entire absence of muscular fatigue, is to a certain extent influenced by the *inclination of the pastern and toe to the cannon. The acute-angled foot,* in the folding of the leg during the first half of the stride, moves through a longer arc of a circle whose centre is the fetlock joint than does the normal or the upright foot; rises more rapidly and to a higher point.

(See Fig. 76, *B*.) When the momentum of a foot moving rapidly and abruptly upward is increased by weight the result is extreme and even exaggerated flexion of all joints of the leg, and by allowing the hoof to grow long the flexion is still further increased. In the show ring, harness horses with fair natural action may be made to " climb " by shoes weighing from thirty to sixty ounces upon hoofs an inch or more longer than normal. The leverage of a heavy shoe on a long hoof is excessive, fatiguing and most injurious to ligament, tendon and muscle. The action, while high, is *labored, pounding* and *altogether inelegant.*

<table>
<tr><td>Fig. 77.</td><td>Fig. 78.</td></tr>
</table>

 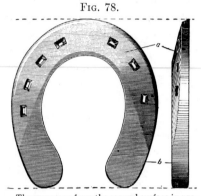

| A 40 oz. right front shoe (hoof-surface) to increase knee-action in a high acting harness horse. For show-purposes only. | The same seen from the ground surface in profile: *a*, bevel from inner border of the web to outer border: *b*, ends of the branches of full thickness from outer to inner border. |

In the training of trotters weight is often used *to increase the length of the stride,* or to cause a *higher folding of a front foot,* in order to prevent " scalping " or " speedy-cut." As soon as the new gait becomes a fixed habit the weight should be gradually lessened. *Weight is carried with less fatigue at a trot* than at a pace, or at a gallop. It therefore steadies a trotter that is inclined to pace, or " break " into a run. The increased momentum of the weighted hoof makes for rhythm of movement, and increases the difficulty of skipping, dwelling, or mixing gaits.

In the base-wide (toe-wide) and *base-narrow* (toe-narrow) *standing positions,* the flight of the hoofs, as seen from in front or behind, is not straight forward, *i.e.,* parallel to the line of progression of the body, but in *arcs of circles.* (See Figs. 72–75, p. 73.) In these cases, increasing the weight of the hoofs, by increasing the momentum, must of necessity increase the tendency of the hoofs to move off at a tangent to the curves which they describe. In other words, *weight increases the centrifugal force* of a body moving in a curve. The *outward swing* of the hoofs of a base-narrow horse (paddling), and the *inward swing* of a base-wide horse (interfering), are made *more pronounced by adding weight to any part of the hoof. The centrifugal force is greatest* in base-wide feet when the weight is on the medial, or inner side of the hoof; in base-narrow feet when it is on the lateral or outer side.

A side weight, or side weight shoe is often of service in a crossfiring pacer. This animal usually stands base-narrow (toe-narrow) behind, and in motion his hind hoofs describe a curve at first forward and outward and then inward till contact is made with the diagonal hoof or leg. The added weight (placed on the outer side) by increasing the centrifugal force carries the hoof just enough farther from the centre around which the hoof swings to prevent contact. (See cross-firing, p. 138.)

Finally, it must not be forgotten that *weight is always weight;* that it *cuts speed* and *devours endurance.*

E. Forms of Hoofs.

A front hoof of the regular standing position (Fig. 79). The inner and outer walls differ but little in direction and thickness. The outer wall is a little thicker and somewhat more slanting than the inner (see Figs. 61 and 62), and its outer circumference describes a larger arc of a circle,—that is, is more curved, as can be seen both at its plantar border and at the coronet. The length of the quarter in relation to the length or height of the side wall and toe is about as 1 : 2 : 3.

The toe forms an angle with the ground of forty-five to fifty
degrees (see Fig. 68). The direction of the wall at the toe,
viewed from the side, should be parallel with the direction of
the long pastern.

A *hoof of the base-wide position* (Fig. 80) *is always awry,*
because the outer wall is
naturally somewhat longer
and decidedly more slant-
ing than the inner (see Figs.
63 and 64). The plantar
border of the outer wall
describes a large arc, whose
sharpest curvature is where
the side wall passes into
the quarter. The plantar
border of the inner wall is
straighter (less curved);
the outer half of the ground
surface (sole) of the hoof
is, therefore, wider than the
inner. So long as the hoof
is healthy, both branches of
the frog are equally developed. The wryness of the
hoof depends upon the di-
rection of the limb; therefore, a base-wide h o o f

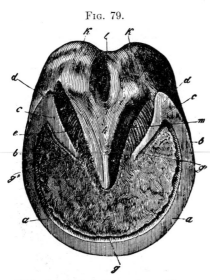

Fig. 79.

Right fore-hoof of the regular position: *a,*
side-wall; *b,* quarter; *c,* beginning of the bar; *d,*
buttress; *e,* middle of the bar; *f,* body of the sole;
f', branches of sole; *g,* white line; *g',* apparent
end of the bar; *h,* body of the frog; *i,* branch of
the fro·; *k,* bulbs (glomes) of the heel; *l,* middle
cleft of frog; *m,* lateral cleft of frog.

should be regarded as a *normally wry hoof,* to distinguish it
from hoofs which are wry from disease.

A *hoof of the toe-wide position* (Fig. 81) is distinguished
from the preceding by the bending or curvature of the plantar
border of the outer toe and inner quarter being often decidedly
less pronounced than on the inner toe and outer quarter; therefore, two short curves and two long curves lie opposite each
other; in other words, the inner toe and outer quarter, lying

opposite each other, are sharply curved, while the outer toe and inner quarter, lying opposite each other, are much less sharply bent or curved. The toes are turned out. The feet are not set down flat upon the ground, but meet it with the outer toe.

A hoof of the base-narrow position is normally wry, but never so pronounced as a hoof of the base-wide position. The inner wall is but little more oblique than the outer, the difference being most noticeable at the quarters (Figs. 65 and 66). The curve of the plantar border of the wall is similar to that of a regular hoof, except that the inner side wall and quarter

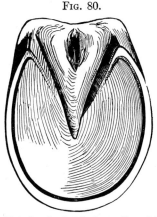

Right fore-hoof of the base-wide position.

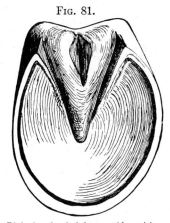

Right fore-hoof of the toe-wide position.

are a little more sharply curved in a base-narrow hoof. Occasionally the outer quarter is somewhat drawn in under the foot.

This form of hoof is most distinctly marked in animals that stand toe-narrow or are bandy-legged.

As to the *forms of the hind hoofs,* what has been said concerning the influence of position of the limbs upon the shape of the front feet will apply equally well to them. The hind hoof (Fig. 82) is not round at the toe, but somewhat pointed or oval. It greatest width is between the middle and posterior thirds of the sole. It usually has a strongly concaved sole and a somewhat steeper toe than the fore-hoof; viewed from the side, the angle of the toe with the ground in the regular standing position is from fifty to fifty-five degrees.

Finally, we also distinguish *wide* and *narrow* hoofs; they are not dependent upon the position of the limbs, but upon the race and breeding of the animal.

The wide hoof (Fig. 83) is almost round upon its plantar surface. Its wall runs quite oblique to the ground. The sole is but moderately concave, and the frog is strong and well developed. *The narrow hoof* (Fig. 84) is rather elliptical, with steep side walls, strongly concaved sole, and small, undeveloped frog. The horn of the narrow hoof is fine and tough; of the wide hoof, usually coarse. The wide hoof may readily become flat. Narrow hoofs are either the result of breeding or premature shoeing.

In enumerating the preceding forms of the hoof we have by no means referred to all the forms in which the hoof may be found; on the contrary, hoofs vary in shape and quality to such an extent that among a hundred horses no two hoofs can be found which are exactly alike. In fact, the same variety exists as in the faces of people, and we know that we can recall in succession even many more faces without finding two that are exactly alike. This explains the manifold differences in horseshoes with respect to size, form and other qualities.

Fig. 82.

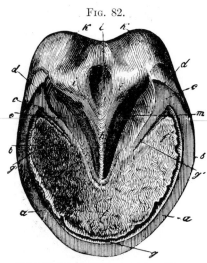

Right hind hoof of the regular position: *a*, side-wall; *b*, beginning of the quarter; *c*, beginning of the bar; *d*, buttress; *e*, middle of bar; *f*, body of the sole; *f'*, branch of sole; *g*, white line of the toe; *g'*, white line of the bar; *h*, body of the frog; *i*, branch of the frog; *k*, bulbs of heel; *l*, middle cleft of frog; *m*, lateral cleft of frog.

Suppose now a hoof is before us; it is first necessary to know whether or not it is **healthy.** Unfortunately, a perfectly healthy hoof is not so easy to find as one may think. We recognize a sound hoof by the following marks: Seen from in front or from the side, the course of the wall from the coronet to the ground, in the direction of the horn-tubes, is straight,—that is, bent neither in nor out. A straight edge, placed upon the wall in the direction of the horn-tubes, touches at every point. The wall must show neither longitudinal nor transverse cracks or

FIG. 83.   FIG. 84.

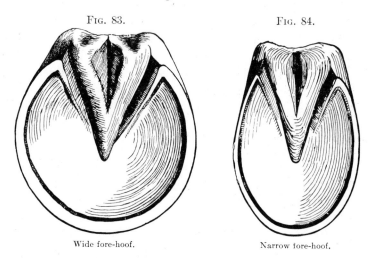

Wide fore-hoof.   Narrow fore-hoof.

fissures. If there be rings, their position and course are important. Rings which pass around the entire circumference of the wall parallel to the coronet indicate nothing more than disturbances of nutrition of the hoof; *but the hoof cannot pass for sound* when the rings have any other position and direction than the one mentioned, or if the rings upon any part of the wall are more marked than elsewhere, even though they may be parallel to the coronary band. Marked ring-building upon the hoofs of horses which have regular feeding, grooming, and work indicates a weak hoof. Viewed from the ground-surface and from behind, the bulbs of the heels should be well rounded, strongly developed, and not displaced. The concave sole should show no separation along the white line. The frog should be strong, well developed, and have symmetrical branches and a broad, shallow, dry median lacuna. The lateral lacunæ of the frog should be clean and not too narrow. The bars should pass in a straight direction forward and inward towards the point of the frog. Any bending outward of the bars towards the branches of the sole indicatès the beginning of a narrowing of the space occupied by the frog,—that is, contraction of the heels. The horn of the branches of the sole in the buttresses and in their proximity should show no red staining. The lateral cartilages should be elastic. No part of the foot should be weakened at the cost of other parts. By firm union of all strong parts the strength and vigor of the hoof is in no sense disturbed. *If one desires to ascertain the exact form and state of health of the hoof, it must never be inspected and judged alone, but in connection with the entire limb.*

F. Growth of the Hoof and Wear of the Hoof and Shoe.

All parts of the horn of the hoof grow downward and forward, the material for this growth being furnished by the remarkably large quantity of blood which flows to the pododerm. The growth of the hoof is regulated by the nerves.

As a rule, the hoof grows **uniformly,**—that is, one section of the wall grows just as rapidly as another. A visible indication of growth is the increase in height and width of the hoof from colthood to maturity.

The *rapidity of growth* of the wall varies, amounting in a month to from one-sixth to one-half of an inch. The average monthly growth in both shod and unshod horses of both sexes is, according to my own experiments, one-third of an inch. Hind hoofs grow faster than front hoofs, and unshod faster than shod. The hoofs of stallions grow more slowly than those of mares and geldings.

Abundant **exercise,** proper grooming (flexibility and moist-ness of the horn), regular dressing of the wall, and **running barefoot** from time to time **favor growth;** while little or no exercise, dryness, and excessive length of the hoof hinder growth.

The time required for the horn to grow from the coronet to the ground is, therefore, equally variable, and is, moreover, dependent upon the height (length of toe) of the hoof. At the toe the horn grows down in from eleven to thirteen months, at the mammæ or sides in from six to eight months, and at the quarters in from three to five months. The time required for the renewal of the entire hoof we term the *period of hoof renewal.* If, for example, we know exactly the rapidity of horn growth in a given case, we can estimate without difficulty the length of the "period of hoof renewal," as well for the entire hoof as for each individual section of the wall. The duration of many diseases of the hoof (cracks, clefts, partial bendings of the wall, contractions, etc.) can be foretold with relative certainty only by knowing the period of hoof renewal.

Irregular growth sometimes takes place. The chief cause of this is usually an improper distribution of the body-weight over the hoof,—that is, an unbalanced foot. Wry hoofs of faulty positions of the limbs are often exposed to this evil; a faulty preparation of the hoof (dressing) for the shoe, as well as neglect of the colt's hoofs, is in the majority of cases directly responsible for this condition.

If in the shortening of the wall a part is from ignorance left too long, or one-half of the hoof shortened too much in relation to the other half, the foot will be unbalanced. The horse will then touch the ground first with the section of wall which has been left too high, and will continue to do so until this long section has been reduced to its proper level (length) by the increased wear which will take place at this point. In unshod hoofs this levelling process takes place rapidly; such, however, is not the case in shod hoofs, for here the shoe prevents rapid wear, and, indeed this levelling process is often rendered impossible through the welding of high steel calks to the shoe. If this fault in trimming be repeated at the next and subsequent shoeings, and if the faulty relation of the ground surface of the hoof to the direction of the foot-axis remain during

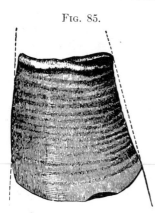

Fig. 85.

Crooked (right) fore-hoof.

several months, the portion of wall left too high will grow more rapidly, the walls will lose their natural straight direction and become bent. If, for example, the outer wall has been left too long during a considerable period of time, a crooked hoof results (Fig. 85) in which the rings are placed closer together upon the low (concave) side than upon the high (convex) side. If for a long time the toe is excessively long, it will become bent; or if this fault affects excessively high quarters they will contract either just under the coronary band or will curl forward and inward at their lower borders. These examples are sufficient to show both the importance of the manner in which a horse places his foot to the ground and its influence upon the loading, growth, and form of the hoof.

Wear of the Shoe and of the Hoof upon the Shoe.

The wear of the shoe is caused much less by the weight of the animal's body than by the rubbing which takes place between the shoe and the earth whenever the foot is placed to the ground and lifted.

The wear of the shoe which occurs when the foot is placed on the ground is termed " **grounding wear**," and that which occurs while the foot is being lifted from the ground is termed " **swinging-off wear**." When a horse travels normally, both kinds of wear are nearly alike, but are very distinct when the

paces are abnormal, especially when there is faulty direction of
the limbs. While in the majority of horses whose limbs have
been stiffened by age and overwork both kinds of wear are most
marked at the toe of the shoe, we see relatively fewer cases of
" grounding wear " at the ends of the branches (as in laminitis) ; on the contrary, we **always** notice "swinging-off wear" at
the toe of the shoe. It is worthy of notice that length of stride
has much to do with the wear. We observe that with shortening of the stride both kinds of wear occur at the toe of the
shoe, and this is rapidly worn away, as is the case with horses

Fig. 86.

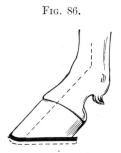

A normal-angled foot
with straight foot axis.
The shoe shows uniform
wear.

Fig. 87.

An upright foot with
foot axis broken forward
by reason of too high quarters. The shoe shows
"grounding" wear at ends
of branches, and "swing-
ing off" wear at toe.

Fig. 88.

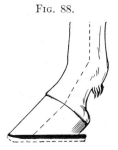

A hoof with foot axis
broken backward by rea-
son of surplus horn at the
toe. The shoe shows ex-
cessive "grounding" and
"swinging off" wear at
the toe.

which are fretful and prance under the rider, draw heavy loads,
or from any other cause, as disease or infirmity, are obliged to
shorten their steps. With increase of length of stride the wear
of the shoe becomes more uniform.

The *position* and *form of the shoe* have a marked influence
upon its wear; **at the place where the shoe is too far under
the hoof** either as a result of shifting or of having been nailed
on crooked, or where the outer branch has not the necessary
width, or does not form a sufficiently large curve, **the wear will
be increased.**

Also the relative length of side-walls, or of toe and heels, influences rapidity of wear of the shoe. If through ignorance or carelessness one side-wall be left too long, the branch beneath will meet the ground before other parts of the shoe and will wear faster (see Figs. 87, 88 and 89).

The wear of the hoof upon the shoe occurs as a result of the movements of the quarters. Visible indications of this are the brightly polished, often sunken places upon the bearing-surface of the ends of the branches, showing that scouring occurs between the horn and the iron. Shoes which show brightly polished places in their anterior halves have been loose. The wear of the quarters upon the shoe is not always uniform, but is usually greater on the inner than on the outer quarter, especially in base-wide feet. The degree of this wear of the hoof may be from nothing to one-fourth of an inch or more from one shoeing to the next. Finally, we should remember that this usually invisible scouring away of the hoof gradually causes the nails at the quarters to become loose, and that this is more clearly marked in the front than in the hind hoofs.

G. Physiological Movements of the Hoof. (Mechanism of the Hoof.)

These movements comprise all those changes of position within and of the hoof which are brought about by alternately weighting and relieving the foot, and which are manifest as changes of form of the hoof. The following changes in form of the hoof are most marked at the time that the hoof bears greatest weight,—that is, *simultaneous* with the greatest descent of the fetlock-joint.

1. A lateral expansion over the entire region of the quarters, occurring simultaneously at the coronary and plantar borders. This expansion is small, and in general varies between one-fiftieth and one-twelfth of an inch.

2. A narrowing of the anterior half of the hoof measured at the coronary border.

3. A decrease in height of the hoof, with a slight sinking of the heels.

4. A flattening (sinking) of the sole, especially in its branches.

These changes of form are much more pronounced in the half of the hoof that bears the greater weight.

A hoof while supporting the body-weight has a different form, and the tissues enclosed within it a different position, than when not bearing weight. Since loading and unloading of the foot are continually alternating, the relations of internal pressure even in the standing animal are continuously changing, so that, strictly speaking, the hoof is never at rest.

The changes in form take place in the following order: the body-weight falls from above upon the os coronæ, os pedis, and navicular bone, and at the moment

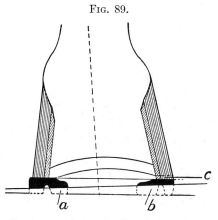

Fig. 89.

Transverse vertical section through the middle of a right fore shod hoof of base-wide form, viewed from behind. The outer wall having been insufficiently lowered has caused increased wear of the underlying branch of the shoe: *a*, wear of inner branch (beneath the relatively short wall); *b*, greater wear of outer branch beneath the relatively long wall; *c*, the horn between the dotted line and the shoe represents the surplus length of this outer wall.

that the foot is placed upon the ground is transmitted through the sensitive laminæ and horny laminæ to the wall. At the instant that the fetlock reaches its lowest point the os pedis bears the greatest weight. Under the body-weight the latter yields, and with the navicular bone sinks downward and backward. At the same time the upper posterior portion of the os coronæ (Fig. 90, *A*) passes backward and downward between the lateral cartilages (*a*), which project above the upper border of the wall, and presses the perforans tendon down upon the plantar cushion. The plantar cushion being compressed from above, and being unable to expand downward, is correspondingly squeezed out towards the sides and crowded against the lateral cartilages, and they, yielding, press against and push before them the wall at the quarters. The resistance of the earth acts upon the plantar surface of the hoof, and especially upon the frog, and it, widening, crowds the bars apart, and in this manner contributes to the expansion of the quarters, especially at their plantar border (see Fig. 90). The horny sole under the descent and pressure

FIG. 90.

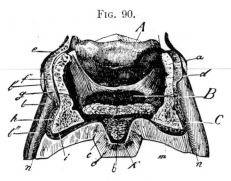

Vertical, transverse section of a foot seen from behind: *A*, os coronæ; *B*, os navicularis; *C*, os pedis; *a*, lateral cartilage; *b*, anterior portion of fleshy frog; *c*, section of perforans tendon; *d*, suspensory ligament of the navicular bone; *l*, wall; *m*, sole; *n*, white line; *o*, frog.

of the os pedis sinks a little—that is, the arch of the sole becomes somewhat flattened. All these changes are much more marked upon *sound unshod* hoofs, because in them the resistance of the earth upon the sole and frog is pronounced and complete. These changes in form are more marked in front feet than in hind. In defective and diseased hoofs it may happen that at the moment of greatest weight-bearing, instead of an expansion a contraction may occur at the plantar border of the quarters.

Three highly elastic organs there are which play the chief part in these movements,—namely, the lateral cartilages, the plantar cushion, and the horny frog. Besides these structures, indeed, all the remaining parts of the horn capsule, especially its coronary border, possess more or less elasticity, and contribute to the above-mentioned changes of form.

In order to maintain the elastic tissues of the foot in their proper activity, regular and *abundant exercise,* with protection against drying out of the hoof, are absolutely necessary, because the movements of the different structures within the foot and the changes of form that occur at each step are indispensable in preserving the health of the hoof. Long-continued rest in the stable, drying out of the hoof, and shoeing decrease or alter the physiological movements of the foot, and these lead under certain conditions to foot diseases, with which the majority of horse owners are entirely unacquainted.

As an outward, visible indication of the mobility of the quarters upon the shoe we may point to the conspicuous, brightly polished, and often sunken spots, or grooves, upon the ends of the branches. They are produced partly by an in-and-out motion of the walls at the quarters, and partly by a forward and backward gliding of the quarters upon the shoe.

The benefits of these physiological movements within the hoof are manifold:

1. Through them shock is dispersed and the body protected from the evil consequences of concussion or shock.

2. These movements increase the elasticity of the entire limb, and in this way contribute much to a light and elegant gait.

3. They maintain a lively circulation of blood in the vessels of the pododerm, and this insures a rapid growth of horn.

Since it is a generally accepted fact that shoeing interferes with the physiological movements of the hoof, alters them, indeed, almost suppresses them, and that all these movements are spontaneous and natural only in sound *unshod* hoofs, we are justified in regarding shoeing as *a necessary evil.* However, it is indispensable if we wish to render horses serviceable upon hard artificial roads. If, in shoeing, consideration be given to the structure and functions of the hoof, and particularly to the hoof-surface of the shoe, the ends of the branches being provided with a smooth, level bearing-surface, which allows free play to the elastic horn capsule, in so far as this is not hindered by the nails we need have no fear of subsequent disease of the hoofs, provided the horse is used with reason and receives proper care.

PART II.

CHAPTER III.

SHOEING HEALTHY HOOFS.

A. Examination of a Horse Preliminary to Shoeing.

An examination should be made while the animal is at rest, and afterwards while in motion. The object of the examination is to gain accurate knowledge of the direction and movements of the limbs, of the form and character of the feet and hoofs, of the manner in which the foot reaches and leaves the ground, of the form, length, position, and wear of the shoe, and distribution of the nail-holes, in order that at the next and subsequent shoeings all ascertained peculiarities of hoof-form may be kept in mind and all discovered faults of shoeing corrected.

The examination is best conducted in the following order: The horse should first be led at a walk in a straight line from the observer over as level a surface as possible, then turned about and brought back, that the examiner may notice the direction of the limbs and the manner in which the hoofs are moved and set to the ground. While the animal is moving away the observer notices particularly the hind limbs, and as it comes towards him he examines the fore-limbs. Then a few steps at a trot will not only show whether or not the animal is lame, but will often remove all doubt in those cases in which, while the animal was walking, the examiner was unable to make up his mind as to which was the predominating position of the limb. The problem presented is, therefore, to determine whether or not the direction of the limbs, the lines of flight of the hoofs, and the manner in which they are set down and picked up are regular. If there are deviations from the normal they will fall either into the base-wide and toe-wide group or into the base-narrow and toe-narrow group. When clear upon these points the horse is allowed to stand quietly, and the observer, placing himself in front, examines the foot more closely, fixes the direction of the foot axis clearly in his mind, marks also the form and character of the hoofs and the position of the coronets, as far as these parts can be inspected from in front. At the same time each hoof should be closely inspected to determine whether the slant of both quarters corresponds to the direction of the long pastern, and whether the course of the wall from the coronet to the plantar border is straight or bent in or out (contraction, fulness). Walls curved from above to below always indicate an unnatural height of some section of the wall and a displacement of the base of support of the foot. In order to gain accurate and complete knowledge of the position of the limbs, the flight of the hoofs, and the manner of setting the foot to the ground, the horse must frequently be moved back and forth many times, especially when the standing position is somewhat irregular and the hoofs are of different shapes.

At this point begins the examination of the position of the limbs, and the form of the feet and hoofs, in profile. After casting a glance over the entire body, so as to gain an idea of the animal's weight, height, and length, the attention is turned to the position and direction of the limbs and hoofs. The eye should particularly note whether the form of the hoof corresponds to the position of the limb, and, furthermore, whether the slant of the pastern is the same as that of the wall at the toe,—that is, whether the foot axis is straight or broken; also whether the toes and quarters are parallel, for the toe is sometimes bulging (convex) or hollowed out (concave) between the coronet and plantar border, and the quarters are frequently contracted and drawn or shoved under the foot (weak quarters). If the wall present rings the observer should note their position with reference to one another and to the coronet, and also their extent, and, furthermore, should determine whether or not they cross one another (thrush of the frog). At the same time he should notice the length of the shoes.

Next, the feet should be raised and the examiner should notice the width of the hoof, the arching of the sole, the character of the frog, the position of the bulbs of the heel, as well as the presence of any cracks or clefts in the wall. Then the old shoes should be examined as to their age, form, the distribution and direction of their nail-holes (" punching "), position, and wear. With respect to the form of the old shoe, one should observe whether or not it corresponds to the form of the hoof. The same careful examination should be made of the number and distribution of the nail-holes. As regards the position of the shoe, one must first ascertain whether it completely covers the bearing-surface of the wall, and whether the shoe extends beyond the wall at any point and has caused interfering or given rise to irregular wear. Finally, the wear of the shoe should be observed, and the following points borne in mind: *One-sided wear, uneven setting down of the feet, and an unnatural course of the wall are often found together*, especially when uneven wearing of the shoe has existed for a long time, —that is, during several shoeings. As a rule, in such a case the more worn branch of the shoe is too near the centre of the foot, and the opposite branch too far from the centre (too " full ") ; in other words, the base of support (shoe) has been shifted too far in the direction of the less worn branch. Moreover, increased wear of a part of a shoe is an indication that the section of the wall above it is too high (too long) (Fig. 89), or that the wall upon the opposite side of the foot is too low (short). The twisting movement of many hind feet should, from physiological reasons, not be hindered by shoeing.

B. Raising and Holding the Feet of the Horse to be Shod.

This can always be done without much trouble if the horse has been accustomed to it from early colthood. Certain rules governing the manner of taking hold of the feet, and of afterwards manipulating them, are of value.

A shoer should **never grasp a foot suddenly,** or with both hands. The horse should first be prepared for this act. First see that the horse stands in such a position that he can bear his weight comfortably upon three legs. This is well worth noticing, and if the horse does not voluntarily assume such an easy position, move him gently until his feet are well under his body.

If the shoer, for example, wishes to raise the left fore foot for inspection, he stands on the left side facing the animal, speaks quietly to him, places the palm of the right hand flat upon the animal's shoulder, and, at the same time, with the left hand strokes the limb downward to the cannon and seizes the cannon *from in front.* With the right hand he now gently presses the horse towards the opposite side, and the foot becoming loose as the weight is shifted upon the other leg, he lifts it from the ground. The right hand now grasps the pastern from the inside followed by the left hand upon the inside and the right hand on the outside; then, turning partly to the right, the holder supports the horse's leg upon his left leg, in which position he should always stand as quietly and firmly as possible. If, now, the shoer desires to have both hands free to work upon the hoof, he grasps the toe with the left hand in such a manner that the toe rests firmly in the palm while the four fingers are closely applied to the wall of the toe, takes a half step toward the rear, passes the hoof behind his left knee into his right hand which has been passed backward between his knees to receive it, and drawing the hoof forward outward and upward supports it firmly on his two knees,—the legs just above the knees being applied tightly against the pastern. The forefoot should not be raised higher than the knee (carpus), nor the hind foot higher than the hock, nor either foot be drawn too far backward. The correct standing position of the shoer or floorman while holding a front foot is shown in Fig. 91. Shortness of stature (5'-5'.6") is desirable in a floorman.

In lifting the *left hind foot* the animal should be gently stroked back as far as the angle of the hip, against which the left hand is placed for support, while the right hand strokes the limb down to the middle of the cannon, which it grasps *from behind.* While the left hand presses the animal's weight over towards the right side, the right hand loosens the foot and carries it forward and outward from the body so that the limb is bent at the hock. The holder then turns his body towards the right, brings his left leg against the anterior surface of the fetlock-joint, and carries the foot backward, at which time his left arm passes over the horse's c r o u p and above and to the inner side of the h o c k. Finally, both hands encompass the long pastern.

If the right feet are to be raised, the process is s i m p l y reversed.

Fig. 91.

Proper position for holding a front foot.

In raising the feet no unnecessary pain should be inflicted by pinching, squeezing, or lifting a limb too high. The wise shoer avoids all unnecessary clamor and disturbance; quiet, rapid, painless methods avail much more. In dealing with *young* horses the feet should not be kept lifted too long; let

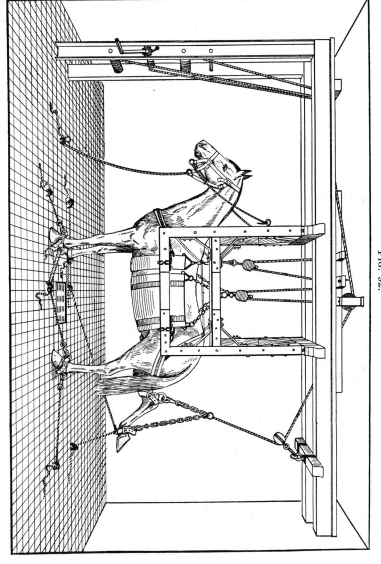

Fig. 92.

The Martin horse rack (modified).

them down from time to time. In *old* and *stiff* horses the
feet should not be lifted too high, especially in the beginning
of the shoeing.

Vicious horses must often be severely handled. Watch
the play of the ears and eyes continually, and immediately
punish every exhibition of temper either by jerking the halter
or bridle vigorously, or by loud commands. If this does not
avail, then if soft ground is at hand make the horse back as
rapidly as possible for some time over this soft surface; it is
very disagreeable and tiresome to him. To raise a hind foot
we may knot a strong, broad, soft, plaited band (side line)
into the tail, loop it about the fetlock of the hind foot, and
hold the end. This often renders valuable service. The
holder seizes the band close to the fetlock, draws the foot
forward under the body, and then holds it as above described. The use of such a band compels the horse to carry
a part of his own weight, and at the same time hinders him
from kicking. Before attempting to place this rope or band
about the fetlock, the front foot on the same side should be
raised.

The various sorts of twitches are objectionable, and their
use should not be allowed unless some painful hoof operation
is to be done. The application of the tourniquet, or " Spanish
windlass," to the hind leg is equally objectionable.

Those horses which resist our attempts to shoe them we
do not immediately cast or place in the stocks, but first have a
quiet, trustworthy man hold them by the bridle-reins and
attempt by gentle words and soft caresses to win their attention
and confidence.

Ticklish horses must be taken hold of boldly, for light
touches of the hand are to such animals much more unpleasant
than energetic, rough handling. Many ticklish horses allow
their feet to be raised when they are grasped suddenly without
any preparatory movements.

C. Removing the Old Shoes.

If a horse's hoofs are healthy, all the shoes may be taken off at the same time, but there are certain diseases of the hoof in which this should not be done.

The rule to follow in removing every shoe is to *draw it cautiously,* not wrench it away with violence. Hoofs which are dirty should first be cleansed, preferably with a stiff brush. Next, the clinches should be *carefully* lifted by means of a rather dull clinch cutter (Fig. 93), *without injuring the horn* of the wall. In order, now, that the nails may be removed singly, the shoe must be slightly lifted. This may be done in one of two ways. The shoer may use a pair of pincers (Fig. 94), with broad bills which will encompass the branch of the shoe and come well together underneath it. The handles of the pincers are then moved *in the direction of the branches* of the shoe. The second method consists in raising the branches of the shoe by driving the nail-cutter from behind between the shoe and hoof and using it as a lever or pry to loosen the shoe.

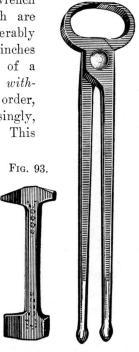

FIG. 94.

FIG. 93.

Clinch cutter
and punch.

Pincers.

Violent and excessive twisting of the hoof and straining of ligaments may easily occur, but the smith should guard against them by supporting the hoof with the left hand or with the leg just above the knee, while loosening the shoe.

D. Preparing the Hoof for the Shoe.

This preparation is usually termed paring, trimming, or dressing. It is a most important step in the process of shoeing, and its object is to shorten the hoof, which has grown too long under the projection of the shoe, and prepare it to receive the new shoe. The instruments needed for this work are the rasp and the hoof-knife (Fig. 95); upon large and hard hoofs a

Fig. 95.

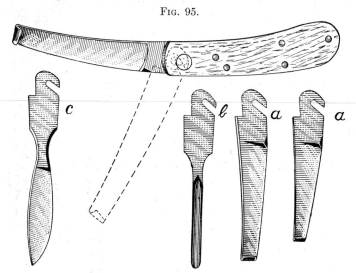

German hoof set with detachable hook blades. (W. M. Kunde, Dresden): *a,a*, hoof blades; *b*, pus searcher; *c*, scalpel.

pair of sharp nippers (Fig. 96), or a sharp **hewing knife, with broad handle and perfectly flat, smooth sides,** may be used, since these instruments will considerably facilitate and hasten the work.

After the shoer has carefully examined the hoofs in the manner described upon pages 90, 91, and 92, and has fixed in mind the relation of the height of the hoofs to the size and weight of the body, he cleanses the hoof and removes all stubs of old

nails. At the same time he should be asking himself *if,
where,* and *how much* horn is to be removed. In all cases all
loosely attached fragments of horn are to be removed, for example, chips of horn produced by repeated bending and stretching of the lower border of the wall. The sole is then freed
from all flakes of dead horn. The shoer then
runs the rasp around the outer border of the
wall and breaks it off to the depth to which
he thinks it should be shortened, and then
**cuts the wall down to its union with the sole,
so that at least one-eighth of an inch of the
edge of the sole lies in the same level as the
bearing-surface of the wall.** Finally, the wall,
white line, and outer margin of the sole, forming the " bearing-surface," must be rasped until
they are perfectly horizontal, except that at the
toe of forehoofs this bearing-surface may be
rasped slightly upward (rolled toe).

Fig 96.

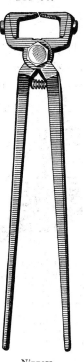

Nippers.

In dressing the hoof the **branches** of the frog
should always be left prominent enough to project beyond the bearing-surface of the quarters
about the thickness of an ordinary flat shoe.
If it be weakened by paring, it is deprived of
its activity, shrinks, and the hoof becomes narrow to a corresponding degree. The frog should,
therefore, be *trimmed* only when it is really *too
prominent.* However, loose and diseased par-
ticles of horn may be trimmed away when it is
affected with thrush.

The *bars* should be spared and never
shortened except when too long. Their union with the wall at
the quarters must in no case be weakened, and never cut through
(opening up the heels). They should be left as high as the
wall at the quarters, or only a little less, while the branches of
the sole should lie about one-eighth of an inch lower.

The *buttress* (angle formed by the union of wall and bar) requires special attention. In healthy unshod hoofs the bars run backward and outward in a straight line from the anterior third of the frog. In shod hoofs, however, it happens that the buttresses gradually lengthen, curl inward, and press upon the branches of the frog, causing the latter to shrink. In such cases the indication is to remove these prolongations of horn from the buttresses so as to restore to the bars their normal direction.

The sharp edge of the plantar border of the wall should be broken away with a rasp until the relative thickness of the wall equals its absolute thickness. (Fig. 97). However, in healthy hoofs, that is, in those whose *walls are straight from the coronet to the ground,* the outer surface of the wall should **never** *be rasped.* The only exceptions to this rule are those cases in which there is an outward bending of the lower edge of the wall, most frequent on the inner side wall and quarter.

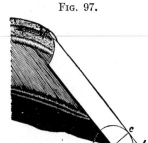

FIG. 97.

Longitudinal (vertical) section of the wall at the toe: *a c* is the absolute, and *a b* the relative thickness of the wall. With *a* as the centre, and the line *a c* as a radius, a circle is drawn; the corner of horn in front of this circle and indicated by dotted lines is to be removed with the rasp.

With respect to the inclination of the ground-surface of the hoof to the direction of the foot axis, as viewed from in front, the following facts are established:

In the *regular* standing position of the limbs (seen from in front) the plantar surface of a hoof is at right angles to the foot axis, and the outer and inner walls are of equal heights.

In the *base-wide* position of the limbs the plantar hoof-surface is more or less inclined to the foot axis, usually to a very small degree, and the outer wall is somewhat higher (longer) and more slanting than the inner.

In the *base-narrow* position of the limbs the plantar hoof-surface is more or less inclined to the direction of the foot axis, usually quite considerably, and the inner wall is somewhat higher than the outer.

The foot is observed from the side in order to determine the proper relation of the length of the toe to the height of the quarters.

In this also the foot axis is our guide. If this axis is as it should be, the wall at the toe and the long pastern will have the **same slant** (Figs. 67, 68 and 69). If the hoof has become too long under the protection of the shoe, this will be shown by the foot axis being no longer a straight line, but broken back-

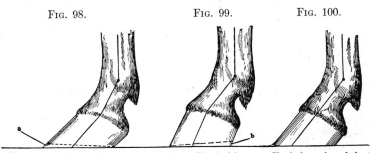

FIG. 98.   FIG. 99.   FIG. 100.

| An untrimmed hoof with an excess of horn (a) at the toe which breaks the foot axis backward. | An untrimmed hoof with an excess of horn (b) at the heels, which breaks the foot axis forward. | Hoof dressed and foot axis straightened by removing excess of horn below dotted lines in the two preceding illustrations. |

ward at the coronet (Fig. 98) ; that is, the hoof in comparison with the fetlock will be too slanting. By shortening the toe more than the quarters this faulty relation will be corrected (Fig. 100) and the foot restored to its proper slant. If the quarters are too long (too high) in comparison with the length of the toe, the foot axis will be broken forward at the coronet (Fig. 99), and the hoof will be too upright. By shortening the quarters more than the toe the foot axis may be made straight. **The plantar surface of the hoof is therefore correct (balanced) when the horse places the foot flat upon the ground in travelling,** and when the lines bounding the hoof, viewed from in front, from behind, and in profile, correspond to the direction of the three phalanges (foot axis).

Finally, this fact should be emphasized, that in changing from flat shoes to those with calks, or the reverse, the hoofs must first be dressed in accordance, so that the foot axes will remain straight, and the feet be set always flat to the ground when the new shoes are on. Each hoof, when ready for the new shoe, should be let down and the horse allowed to stand upon it while it is again carefully examined and closely compared with the opposite hoof. Only after such close inspection has proved the dressing to be faultless can the hoof be considered as properly prepared and ready for the shoe. *The two front hoofs and the two hind hoofs, when the legs are in the same position, should not only be of equal size, but also in proper relation to the size and weight of the body.*

E. Preparing the Hoof for going Barefoot.

This becomes necessary when the nature of the ground and the kind of service required of the horse render shoeing unnecessary. However, to go barefoot the hoof must have **plenty of horn.** After removing the shoes **the frog should be pared down nearly to the level of the wall,** and the sharp outer edge of the wall **well rounded** off with the rasp, in some cases as far as the white line, otherwise large pieces of the wall will readily break away. Hoofs with very slanting walls must be more strongly rounded off than upright hoofs. Going barefoot strengthens the hoofs. From time to time the condition of these shoeless hoofs should be ascertained by inspection, and any growing fault in shape or direction of the horn immediately corrected. It quite frequently happens that the sharp edge of the wall must be repeatedly rounded, especially on very oblique walls (outer half of base-wide hoofs), and the quarters may require frequent shortening, because they are not always worn away as fast as the horn at the toe.

F. Making Shoes.*

Besides good, tough iron for the shoe, we need an anvil with a round horn and a small hole at one end, a round-headed turning-hammer, a round sledge, a stamping hammer, a pritchel of good steel, and, if a fullered shoe is to be made, a round fuller. Bodily activity and, above all else, a good eye for measurement are not only desirable, but necessary. A shoe should be made thoughtfully, but yet quickly enough to make the most of the heat.

The iron of which horseshoes are made is derived from the natural iron ore. Iron used for technical purposes is not chemically pure. Pure iron is rather too soft, and is therefore mixed with different substances, mostly with " carbon," the most important ingredient of our fuel. Of course, the iron contains a very small quantity of carbon (0.5 to 5 per cent.). When iron contains more than 2.3 per cent. of carbon it is hard, brittle, and more easily melted, and is known as crude iron, or raw iron, because it is derived from the raw product, —black ore. The melted crude iron is called *cast iron*. Iron is ductile when it contains less than 2.3 per cent. of carbon, and is then called forge iron, or *wrought iron*. Wrought iron is fusible only at a high temperature. Only weldable iron containing less than 1.6 per cent. of carbon is suitable for general use. Of this iron we distinguish two sorts,—steel and wrought iron. A larger percentage of carbon is found in steel

---

* On a shoe we distinguish an *outer* and an *inner branch*. The anterior portion, formed by the union of the two branches, is called the *toe*. The upper surface, upon which the hoof rests, is called the *hoof-surface*, and the under surface, which is in contact with the ground, the *ground-surface*. That portion of the hoof-surface which is in direct contact with the lower border of the wall, the white line, and a narrow margin of the sole is termed the *bearing-surface*, and when necessary " concaving " (seating) extends from this to the inner border of the shoe. On the ground-surface is seen the " fullering " or " crease."

than in wrought iron. Steel is hard, can be tempered, and may be called tempered wrought iron. In order to temper or harden steel, bring it to a cherry-red heat, and then cool it suddenly by dipping it in cold water or wet sand. The tempered steel can again be softened as desired by heating and slowly cooling. By heating to a high temperature in a forge wrought iron will become doughy, and may then be intimately united (welded) with another piece at the same temperature by pressure or hammering. This property is called weldability; it is of great importance in making horse-shoes. The heating of iron until it reaches the welding stage is called getting a "heat." The act of welding wrought iron with steel is called "steeling."

Regarding **the tools,** the following hints are sufficient:

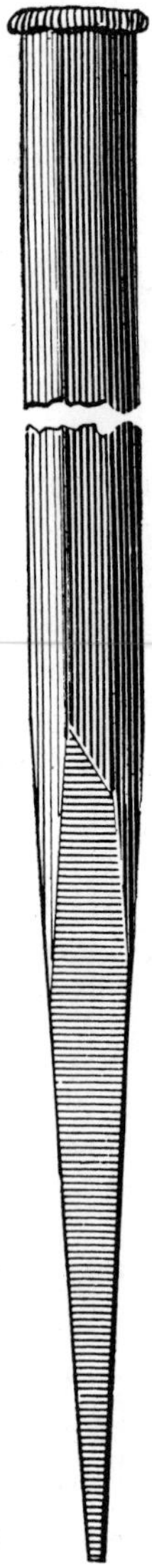

The *anvil* should have a level, smooth, flat steel face.

Likewise, the round head and flat face of both *turning-hammer* and *sledge* should be smooth.

On the *fullering-hammer* (Fig. 101) the left side is flat, the right side convex, and the cutting edge has slightly rounded corners.

FIG. 103.

FIG. 101.

FIG. 102.

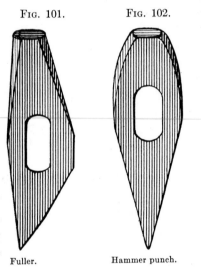

Fuller.

Hammer punch.

Pritchel.

The *hardy, fullering-hammer,* and *cold chisel* should be flawless on the edge.

The *punch* (Fig. 102), used to make the nail-holes in the shoe, has a dull point, which should correspond in size with the head of the horseshoe-nail and have slightly rounded corners.

The *pritchel* (Fig. 103) should not taper to a point, but should end in a rectangular surface whose length is twice its width, in order to punch iron through the shoe under the blow of the hammer.

Making the Shoe.

To make a flat shoe, take the length of the hoof from the point of the toe to the buttress and the greatest width of the hoof; these two measurements, when added together, give the length of the bar for the shoe. The bar should be of such width and thickness as will require the least amount of working. For a bar-shoe or a shoe with heel-calks the bar must be correspondingly longer.

Should we wish to preserve the exact outline of the plantar border of the wall, we may advantageously use such a *podometer* as is shown in Fig. 104. This consists of a perforated sheet-iron plate one-sixteenth to one-twelfth of an inch thick. This is laid upon the hoof, and the outline of the wall marked upon it with chalk.

If necessary, the hoof may be set on a piece of smooth, stiff wrapping paper or card-board, and the outline of the wall closely traced with a lead pencil.

To make a **front shoe** (Figs. 107 and 108), heat the bar white-hot just beyond its middle, place the head of the sledge hammer across one end of the face of the anvil, hold the unheated end of the bar on the head of the sledge,—the heated end resting on the face of the anvil, and bend the bar into a half-circle with the round head of the turning-hammer. (The outer branch of all shoes is made first; in making pairs the right shoe is made first.) The extreme end of the heated bar is drawn out to the desired width and thickness with the sledge. The bent branch is then placed obliquely across the heel of the horn of the anvil, is turned over toward the right

till it rests upon an edge, and is then bevelled diamond-shaped
from the toe to the end of the branch. [The edge in contact
with the horn is the inner edge of the right branch (outer
branch) of the right shoe; the edge beaten down by the hammer
is the outer edge of the outer branch.] The branch is then
flattened on the anvil because in the bending the outer edge
has been stretched and thinned, while the iron of the inner
edge has been crowded together (back-set) and thickened. In

flattening, the shoe should be left

FIG. 104.

Podometer.

a trifle thinner on the inner edge.
The branch is again placed over
the horn, and gone over lightly
with the flat head of the turning-
hammer and brought to a proper
shape. It is now to be concaved
with or without the help of the
sledge, or the concaving may be
omitted. The concaving should
end about three-fourths of an
inch from the end of the branch.
Now turn the branch and fuller
it, or fuller it first and concave
afterwards. The fuller should
be set in about one-twelfth of
an inch from the edge for small
shoes, somewhat more for large shoes, and led from the end of
the branch towards the toe, twice being necessary to make the
fullering of sufficient depth. Next, stamp the holes, punch
them through with the pritchel, run over the surfaces, go over
the outer edge of the shoe upon the horn, and, finally, hammer
the bearing-surface smooth and horizontal. The left branch is
made in the same way, except that it is turned to the left and
the fullering carried from the toe to the heel. **Any ordinary
shoe can and should be completed in the rough in two heats.**
One pair of shoes requires from eight to fifteen minutes.

The **hind shoe** (Fig. 116) is made in like manner, but the branches are not bent in a circle but given that form shown in Fig. 106. Concaving is not necessary; it is sufficient merely to round the inner edge of the web.

FIG. 105.   FIG. 106.

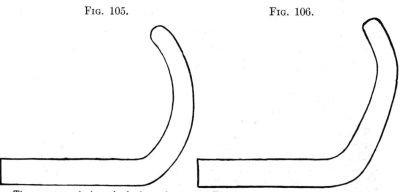

The curvature of a branch of a front shoe.   The curvature of a branch of a hind shoe.

Since in bending the shoe, and especially the toe of a hind shoe, the inner edge is crowded together (back-set) and thickened to the same extent that the outer edge is stretched and thinned, we must remember to do away with these inequalities of thickness and strain by hammering the shoe smooth.

Peculiarities of the Shoe.

They are dependent upon the structure, direction, and position of the leg and hoof, as well as upon the horse's service and the nature of the ground. Since the shoe is an artificial base of support, and since a proper surface of support is of the greatest importance in preserving the soundness of the feet and legs, careful attention must be given to this matter. Naturally shoes designed for the various forms of hoofs must present equally great and equally numerous differences of form, as well as other peculiarities.

General Properties. 1. Form.— A form corresponding to the shape of the hoof is indispensable in every shoe. Front and hind and right and left shoes should be sharply defined and easily distinguishable. *Front shoes* must, above all else, be circular *round at the toe. Hind shoes,* on the contrary, should be *round pointed at the toe,* yet not too much so, but as in Fig. 116.

2. **Width.**—All shoes should be wider webbed (more covered) at the toe than at the ends of the branches. The medium width should be about twice the thickness of the wall.

3. **Thickness.**—Each shoe should, in general terms, be so thick that it need not be renewed under four weeks. Lungwitz

FIG. 107.   FIG. 108.

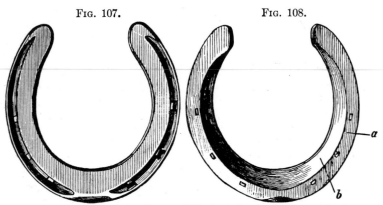

Right front shoe, ground-surface.   Right front shoe, hoof-surface: *a,* bearing-surface; *b,* concaving, or "seating."

found that the average required thickness is about seven-sixteenths of an inch. Of course, this thickness must be diminished or increased according to the rapidity of wear of the shoe. *Shoes without calks should be of uniform thickness,* unless there are special reasons for making them otherwise.

4. **Length.**—For draft-horses they should be long enough to reach the bulbs of the heel, otherwise shorter, though in other respects they may differ (see " special properties "), but should in all cases completely cover the bearing-surface of the hoof.

5. **Surfaces.**—That part of the hoof-surface of the shoe which is in contact with the hoof (bearing-surface of the shoe,

Fig. 109, *a*) should be horizontal and wide enough to cover the wall, the white line, and from a twelfth to an eighth of an inch of the outer edge of the sole. Shoes for large hoofs require a broader bearing-surface than those for small hoofs. The concaving, or "seating" (Fig. 109, *b*), should be made deeper or shallower, according to the nature of the sole. *Shoes for hoofs with strongly arched* (very concave) *soles, do not require any concaving* (hind hoofs, narrow fore-hoofs). *The object of concaving is to prevent pressure of the shoe upon the horny sole except at its margin.*

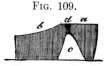

FIG. 109.

Transverse section of a branch of a front shoe: *a*, bearing-surface; *b*, concaving; *c*, fullering, or "crease"; *d*, nail-hole.

The ground-surface of the shoe should be flat and *perfectly horizontal*, except at the toe, which may be turned upward (rolled toe, "rolling motion").

6. **Borders.**—The *outer border* should usually be moderately *base-narrow*,—that is, the circumference of the ground-surface of the shoe should be less than the circumference of its hoof-surface; in other words, the entire outer border of the shoe should be bevelled under the foot. Shoes made base-narrow are not so easily loosened, and materially assist in preventing interfering. The *inner border* should be moderately rounded.

FIG. 110.

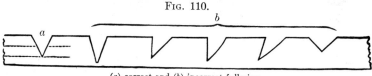

(*a*) correct and (*b*) incorrect fullering.

7. **The "Fullering"** (Fig. 109, *c*).—In depth it should be about two-thirds the thickness of the shoe, of uniform width, and "clean." A fullering is not absolutely necessary, but it makes the shoe lighter in proportion to its size, facilitates a uniform placing of the nail-holes, renders the ground-surface somewhat rough, and, because it is rather difficult to make, increases the workman's skill.

8. **Nail-Holes** (Fig. 109, *d*).—**The importance of the nail-holes,** as regards their *character, number, distribution, depth,* and *direction,* **cannot be over-estimated,** because by the nails which are driven through them the stability of the shoe upon the hoof should be maintained without injuring the sensitive structures, splitting the horny wall, or immoderately interfering with the elasticity of the foot. Each nail-hole should taper uniformly from the ground to the hoof-surface (funnel-shaped). For a medium-weight shoe six nail-holes are sufficient, while for all heavy shoes, especially those with toe- and heel-calks,

FIG. 111.   FIG. 112.

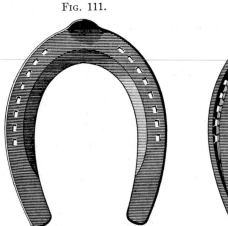

Swiss military shoe, hoof-surface.   Swiss military shoe, ground-surface.

eight are indicated; however, it should by no means be said that every nail-hole should contain a nail. Hind shoes usually require one more nail-hole than front shoes, yet seldom more than eight. In front shoes the nail-holes should be placed in the anterior half of the shoe (Figs. 107 and 108), while in hind shoes they are to be placed in the anterior two-thirds of the shoe (Fig. 116), and in both cases so distributed that the toe shall be without nail-holes, except in those shoes in which it may be desirable to omit the nail-holes in an entire branch

(Fig. 153). **The depth of the nail-holes**—that is, their distance from the outer edge of the shoe—will depend always upon the thickness of the wall, and **should equal the absolute** (real) **thickness of the wall** (Fig. 97). It is evident, therefore, that all nail-holes should not be placed at the same depth (for thickness of the wall, see p. 53).

The **direction** in which the nail-holes should pass through the shoe depends upon the obliquity of the wall. The nail-holes around the toe, as a rule, should incline somewhat in-

FIG. 113.

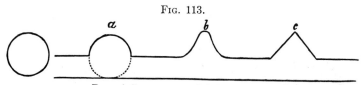

Form of clips: *a*, correct; *b*, indifferent; *c*, faulty.

ward, the holes at the sides less so, while those at the quarters should be punched straight,—that is, should pass perpendicularly through the shoe.

Both front and hind shoes for army horses in time of war and manœuvres should be so punched that one or two nails may be placed in the posterior half of the shoe (Figs. 111 and 112).

9. **Clips** (Fig. 113) are *half-circular, leaf-like ears* drawn upward from the outer edge of the shoe. They should be strong and without flaw at the base, and somewhat **higher and thicker** upon hind than upon front shoes. Their height on flat shoes should equal the thickness of the shoe, while on shoes with leather soles, or with toe- and heel-calks they should be somewhat higher.

According to their position we distinguish toe- and side-clips. They secure the shoe against shifting; therefore, as a rule, every shoe should have a toe-clip. A side-clip should always be drawn up on that branch of the shoe which first meets the ground in locomotion.

A Shoe with Heel-Calks.—All shoes with heel-calks designed for healthy hoofs should be so made and applied that they will disturb the normal setting down of the foot as little as possible, that the wear of the shoe will take place uniformly, and slipping be diminished. The toe of the shoe must, therefore, be left s o m e w h a t

Fig. 114.

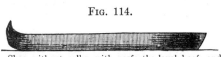

Shoe without calks, with perfectly level hoof- and ground-surfaces, and with roll at the toe (flat, rolling-motion shoe).

Fig. 115.

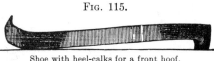

Shoe with heel-calks for a front hoof.

t h i c k e r than the branches just in front of the heel-calks. Moreover, every front shoe with heel-calks must be relatively long, and be provided with considerable rolling motion at the toe; that is, the shoe should be turned up at the toe, the bending beginning near the inner edge of the web. The three- or four-cornered, somewhat conical heel-calks with rounded corners should not be higher than the thickness of the shoe. With reference to the direction of the ends of the branches, we should see to it that they do not rise excessively, but that they assume as near as possible a horizontal direction in passing back to the heels (see Fig. 115).

A Shoe with Toe- and Heel-Calks.—Such a shoe should be of uniform thickness from end to end, and should have a toe-calk and two heel-calks that are somewhat stronger and longer than the heel-calks of a shoe which has no toe-calk. If to a shoe of uniform thickness, on which the heel-calks are somewhat higher than those already described, a piece of steel (Fig. 116, b) of the height of the heel-calks is welded at the toe, we have a shoe with toe- and heel-calks. The toe-calk should never be higher than the heel-calks. There are three principal kinds of toe-calks,—namely:

1. *The Sharp Toe-Calk.*—A bar of toe-steel of proper width and thickness for the toe-calk is thrust with the shoe into the

fire. When the end of the bar is cherry-red in color it is withdrawn, laid across the straight hardy, and cut nearly through
at a point a calk-length from the end. Bar and shoe are then
brought to a welding heat, the calk quickly and securely welded
across the toe of the shoe, the bar wrenched away, the calk gone
over again with the hammer, when it is immediately beaten out
to a sharp edge from the anterior face, either over the far edge
of the anvil, or in a foot-vise. The posterior face of a sharp
toe-calk should be perpendicular to the ground-surface of the
shoe. Machine-made toe-calks,—sharp, half-sharp and blunt,
provided with a sharp spud at one or both ends, are in general
use. Their use requires
two heats, and the sharp
calk is blunted in the
welding.

FIG. 116.

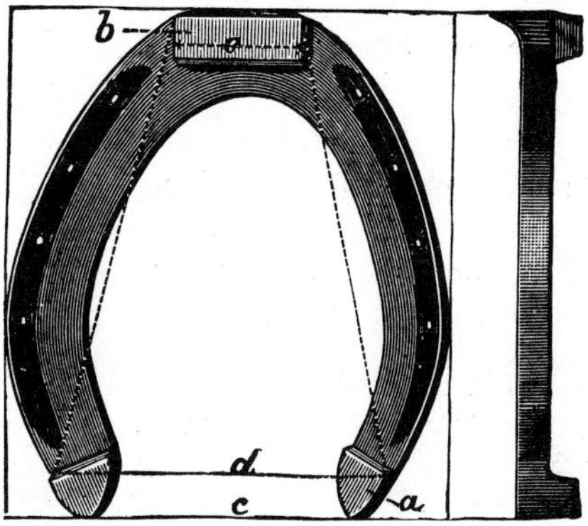

2. *The Blunt Toe-
Calk.*—It is a rather long
rectangular piece of toe-
steel, straight, or curved to
conform to the toe of the
shoe. The shoe-surface
and the ground-surface of
the calk are of equal di-
mensions. It should be
welded on in one heat.

Right hind shoe with toe- and heel-calks: *a,* heel-
calks; *b,* toe-calk; *c,* greatest width of the base of
support (*i.e.,* contact with the ground) of this shoe
when *without* toe- and heel-calks; *d,* the greatest,
and *e,* the least width of the base of support of this
shoe with calks.

3. *T h e Half-Sharp
Toe-Calk* (Coffin-Lid Toe-
Calk).—It resembles the
blunt calk, except that the surface of the calk that is applied
to the shoe is somewhat broader and longer than the surface that comes in contact with the ground. It is welded on
in one heat. The first and third kinds are most suitable for
winter.

Since heel- and toe-calks raise the hoof far from the ground
and prevent all pressure upon the frog, they diminish the

elasticity of the hoof and injure it. They are injurious also to the joints, because they furnish a base of support which is essentially smaller than that afforded by a flat shoe (Fig. 116). However, they are indispensable for heavy draft purposes on *slippery* roads and in winter. Upon all other roads and in summer they are superfluous, at least upon front hoofs, especially as they do not wholly prevent slipping.

Special Properties.—The many different forms of hoofs require a great variety of shoes. Following are the special peculiarities of each of the chief classes of shoes.

1. *Shoe for a Regular Hoof.*—Outer edge: moderately base-narrow (bevelled under) all around. Distribution and direction of the nail-holes: regular. Length: longer than the hoof by the thickness of the shoe (see Figs. 121 and 122).

2. *Shoe for an Acute-Angled Hoof.*—Outer edge: strongly base-narrow around the toe, but gradually becoming perpendicular towards the ends of the branches. Punching: regular, except that the nail-holes at the toe must incline inward somewhat more than usual. Length: rather longer than the preceding shoe (see Fig. 123).

3. *Shoe for an Upright* (stumpy) *Hoof.*—Outer edge: perpendicular at the toe; but if the hoof is very steep, then base-wide at the toe,—*i.e.,* bevelled downward and outward. Punching: last nail should be placed just beyond the middle of the shoe. Direction of the holes: perpendicular. Length: short; at most, one-eighth of an inch longer than the hoof. In the case of a " bear-foot " (see Fig. 70) the shoe should be long.

4. *Shoe for a Base-Wide Hoof.*—Outer edge; the outer branch should be moderately base-narrow,—*i.e.,* bevelled downward and inward, the inner branch perpendicular. Punching: upon the outer branch the holes should extend well back, while upon the inner branch they are to be crowded forward towards the toe (see Fig. 117). Length will depend upon the obliquity of the hoof as seen in profile (see 1, 2, and 3).

5. *Shoe for a Base-Narrow Hoof.*—Outer edge: the outer branch either perpendicular or base-wide, the inner branch

strongly base-narrow. Punching: the nail-holes in the outer branch should be crowded towards the toe and, under certain conditions, punched deeper than the wall is thick, on account of the greater width of this branch; in the inner branch the nail-holes are to be distributed back to the quarter and punched light (see Fig. 118). Length will depend upon the obliquity of the hoof. The outer branch should be about one-fourth of an inch longer than the inner.

6. *Shoe for a Wide Hoof.*—Somewhat wider webbed (more

FIG. 117.

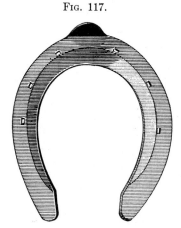

A right front shoe for a base-wide (toe-wide) hoof. The inner branch should be about one-fourth of an inch longer than the outer.

FIG. 118.

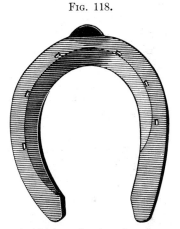

A right front shoe for a base-narrow (toe-narrow) hoof. The outer branch is wider and one-fourth of an inch longer than the inner.

covered) than usual. Outer edge: bevelled under the foot all around (base-narrow). Punching: nail-holes carried back into the posterior half of the shoe (see Fig. 119). Length will depend upon the obliquity of the hoof.

7. *Shoe for a Narrow Hoof.*—Outer edge: moderately bevelled under the foot at the toe (base-narrow), elsewhere perpendicular. Distribution of the nail-holes: regular. Direction of the nail-holes: perpendicular and towards the quarters, inclining somewhat outward. The holes about the toe incline

somewhat inward.   Length will depend upon the obliquity of
the hoof.   Concaving unnecessary (see Fig. 120).

The forms of shoes described in paragraphs 2 to 7 differ
from that described in paragraph 1, but are necessary in order
to lessen the injurious consequences of irregular loading (un-
balancing) of the feet, and of unfavorable bases of support of
the body-weight.

FIG. 119.

FIG. 120.

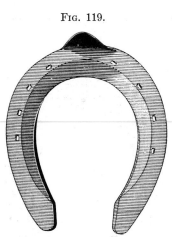

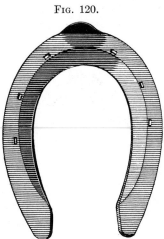

Flat shoe for a round hoof (right front).

A left front shoe for a narrow hoof.   The
concaving is unnecessary.

G. Choosing the Shoe.

The choice of the shoe for a given horse is not at all difficult
after we have carefully considered his weight, the nature of his
work, his standing position, gait, the form of his hoofs, and
quality of the horn, bearing in mind the general and peculiar
properties of shoes.   As a rule, we choose a shoe that is longer
than the hoof, because the latter grows and carries the shoe
forward with it, and because the quarters gradually become
lowered by rubbing and wearing away upon the branches of
the shoe.   The **length** of the shoe is of especial importance.
For horses employed for slow, heavy-draft purposes the shoe
supplied with heel- and toe-calks should extend backward far

enough to support the bulbs of the heels. On the contrary, horses used at a trot or gallop, as coach- and saddle-horses, require shorter shoes (see Fig. 124).

The *weight* of the shoe should be so adjusted to the demands of the horse's work, the condition of the legs (whether used up with work or not), and the nature of the ground that the shoeing will last *at least a month.* Hard roads and a heavy, clumsy gait require strong, durable shoes, which, under some conditions, are to be rendered still more durable by welding in steel. For moderate service upon soft roads we should use light shoes. Running horses require unusually thin and narrow shoes of steel (see Figs. 125–128).

H. Shaping and Fitting Shoes. General Considerations.

This is one of the most important parts of horseshoeing. Its object is to so fashion or shape the shoe which has been chosen for a particular hoof that its circumference will exactly correspond to the lower circumference of the previously prepared hoof, and its bearing-surface will fit air-tight to the bearing-surface of the hoof. At this time all defects in the surfaces of hoof and shoe and in the nail-holes must be remedied, the clips drawn up, and the shoe made to fit perfectly. The bearing-surface of the shoe, especially at the ends of the branches, must be kept **horizontal*** and smooth, and its width regulated by the width of the bearing surface of the hoof (see page 99). Perfectly *uniform heating* is absolutely indispensable in shaping the shoe, because an irregularly heated shoe twists or becomes distorted at the warm places. Every shoe should be straight, and when held before the eye one branch should exactly cover the other. A flat shoe laid upon a level surface should touch at all parts of its ground-surface; the only exception to

---

* The horizontal bearing-surface is in accordance with nature, because the changes of form of the hoof which take place at the plantar border of the wall, on burdening and unburdening the foot, should not be interfered with. A horizontal bearing-surface best fulfils this requirement.

this is the shoe with a rolled toe (rolling motion), in which the toe is turned upward. A shoe is termed *" trough-shaped "* when only the inner edge of the web rests upon the flat surface. It is faulty, disturbs the stability of the foot, and shifts the weight of the body too much upon the quarters.

To front shoes we give a **rolled toe** (Fig. 121, rolling motion), by which we mean a more or less pronounced upward turn of the toe of the shoe. Ordinarily, the toe begins to turn up at the middle of the web, and should be elevated about one-half the thickness of the iron. The rolled toe corresponds to

FIG. 121.

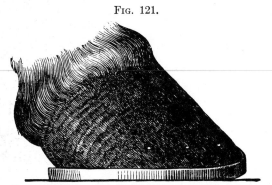

Shod fore-hoof viewed in profile to show the "roll" at the toe.

the natural wear of front hoofs, facilitates the " breaking over " of the feet, and insures a uniform wear of the shoe (see Fig. 86). The shoe is made moderately hot and placed on the foot with the toe-clip against the wall exactly in front of the point of the frog. The scorched horn should be repeatedly removed with the rasp until a perfect-fitting bed has been made upon the bearing-surface of the hoof. From the bearing-surface of the shoe to the inner border of the web the iron must be free from the sole around its entire circumference. The horn sole should not be burnt, because the velvety tissue of the sole lies immediately above it. In the region of the nail-holes the outer borders of shoe and wall should correspond. **The nail-holes**

must under all conditions cover the white line. From the last
nail-hole back to the ends of the branches, for hoofs of the
regular standing position of the limbs, the shoe should gradually
widen until it projects at each quarter from a sixteenth to an
eighth of an inch beyond the edge of the wall. The posterior
half of the shoe should, therefore, be somewhat wider than the
hoof. The effect of this will be to prolong the usefulness of the
shoes. With respect to the *width of the branches,* an exception
arises in the case of *hind*
shoes, in which the inner
branch, with few exceptions,
should closely follow the border of the wall; this will prevent interfering and tearing
off the shoe by the opposite
foot.

Fɪɢ. 122.

Between the ends of the
branches and the frog there
should be enough room, with
few exceptions, to pass a
foot-pick.

In order to judge of the
width of a shoe which has
been fitted to the hoof, it is
of advantage to seize the hoof

Left fore-hoof of normal position shod.

in the left hand and, extending it towards the ground, to
observe from behind and above the outer border of the shoe
and the surfaces of the wall.

*Furthermore, the most important rule is that the shoe should
always have the form of the foot, so long as the form of the hoof
remains unaltered. In all hoofs that have already undergone
change of form we must strive to give the shoe that form which
the hoof had before it underwent change.* Such treatment will
not only do the hoof no injury, but, on the contrary, is of
advantage to it, as it is well known that in time the hoof will
acquire the form of the shoe.

Shaping and Fitting Shoes. Special Considerations.

(*a*) *A shoe for a hoof of the regular form fits properly* when the outer border of the shoe in the region of the nail-holes closely follows the outer edge of the wall, but from the last nail-hole to the end of each branch extends beyond the wall from a sixteenth to an eighth of an inch, the shoe is straight, lies firmly and air-tight upon the bearing-surface of the hoof, the nail-holes fall exactly upon the white line, and there is sufficient space between the frog and the branches of the shoe for the passage of a foot-pick. The branches must be of equal length.

While in fitting a shoe to a hoof of regular form we need pay attention only to the form of the hoof, *it is very different when we come to shape and fit shoes to hoofs of irregular forms. In these cases we must consider not only the form of the hoof, but the position of the limbs and the distribution of weight in the hoof,* because **where the most weight falls the surface of support of the foot must be widened, and where least weight falls (on the opposite side) the surface of support must be narrowed.** In this manner the improper distribution of weight within the hoof (an unbalanced foot) is regulated,—that is, is evenly distributed over the surface of support. The manner in which this is accomplished in the various forms of hoofs is as follows:

(*b*) *An acute-angled hoof* requires the shoe described in paragraph 2, page 114. The branches must be long, because more of the weight falls in the posterior half of the foot, and long branches extend the surface of support backward, while the surface of support in front is to be diminished by making the toe of the shoe base-narrow, either by turning it up or by bevelling it in under the foot. A shoe for an acute-angled hoof fits when it is otherwise related to the hoof as is described in paragraph *a,* above.

(*c*) *An upright or stumpy hoof* presents exactly reverse conditions with respect to the distribution of weight within the hoof, and is treated in an exactly opposite manner. The surface of support should be increased at the toe and diminished at the quarters. This is accomplished by a shoe possessing the peculiarities described in paragraph 3, page 114, whose nail-holes are directed either straight or slightly outward.

(*d*) *A base-wide hoof* requires the surface of support to be widened upon the inner side of the foot and narrowed upon the outer side, because the inner half of the foot bears the more weight. A shoe having the peculiarities described in paragraph 4, page 114, accomplishes this end.

(*e*) *The base-narrow hoof* is just the reverse of the preceding, and requires a shoe whose peculiarities are described in paragraph 5, page 114. While in the normal standing position

FIG. 123.

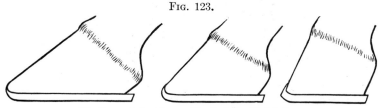

The three principal forms of hoofs shod with flat shoes.

of the limbs, viewed from in front, the ends of the branches of the shoe should be equally distant from the middle of the median lacuna of the frog, this is not so in the base-wide and base-narrow positions. In the base-wide position the outer and in the base-narrow position the inner branch should be somewhat farther from the median lacuna than the branch of the opposite side.

(*f*) *The wide hoof* has too large a surface of support, and, therefore, the shoe designed for it should possess the peculiarities enumerated in paragraph 6, page 115.

(*g*) *The narrow hoof* has already too narrow a base of support, and must not be made smaller; therefore, the shoe should not have a base-narrow but a perpendicular outer border, as described in paragraph 7, page 115.

Shoeing Saddlers and Hunters.

The shoes for saddlers (Park Hacks) should be light, short, and fitted snug to prevent forging, interfering and pulling of the shoes. The hoof surface should cover the wall, white line and at least one-fourth of an inch of the margin of the sole. An average width of one inch is desirable. Both front and hind shoes should be fullered and concaved on the ground surface (convex iron). **The Front Shoe:**—*Length,* should not project beyond the buttress more than one-eighth of an inch. *Width,*

Fig. 124.

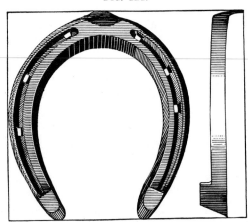

A right front shoe with forging calks; suitable for a saddle horse, or hunter (convex iron).

an inch at the middle on the branches, somewhat more at the toe, and less at the ends of the branches. *Bevelling,* outer-border, base-narrow all around. The ends of the branches, and the heel calks, in case they are used, are bevelled strongly downward and forward under the foot. The toe is rolled from the inner edge of the web, and provided with a strong central clip. Six nails are sufficient (see Fig. 124).

The Hind Shoe:—*Length,* the shoe may project from one-fourth to three-eighths of an inch behind the buttresses. The toe should be well rounded and somewhat blunt so that the horn of the toe will project beyond the shoe an amount equal to one-half the thickness of the wall. *Width,* somewhat less than the front shoe. The branches are of equal thickness, and should carry heel calks whose height equals the thickness of the shoe. To guard against interfering the inside calk may be omitted and the inner branch thickened, fitted snug and bevelled strongly base-narrow. Clips are to be placed at inner and outer toes. Seven nails are sufficient.

The shoes for hunters do not differ materially from those suitable for Park Hacks. The hunter's shoes are somewhat lighter, and to guard against injury to the feet by over-reaching and interfering, and against the shoes being pulled by stiff mire and by treading, the shoes must represent merely a prolongation of the hoofs, *i.e.,* must be no longer and no wider than the hoofs themselves. **The front shoe** of narrow, convex iron is rolled at the toe and has a central toe clip. Forging heel calks are advisable.

The hind shoe is set back at the toe, carries inner and outer toe clips, an outer heel calk and an inner interfering branch. Seven nails.

Shoeing Runners.

Racing plates are intended solely to prevent excessive wear and breaking away of the wall, and to insure a secure foothold upon the ground. The shoes are made as light as possible, but they must not be so narrow and thin that they will bend or break. They are therefore made of steel, wide enough to cover the bearing surface of the wall, white line, and an eighth of an inch of the sole. The ground surface is divided into two sharp edges by a deep, clean, fullering continued entirely around the shoe. Heel calks are of no advantage. Front and hind shoes carry six nails. The last nails are well back in the quarters to prevent the spreading or bending of the light shoe. Front shoes are provided with central toe-clips; hind shoes carry inner and outer toe clips and are set slightly under at the toe (see Figs. 125, 126, 127, 128). An *average weight* running plate for a medium-sized hoof is *three to four ounces.*

FIG. 125.

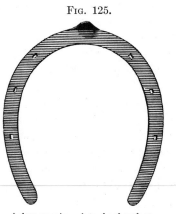

A fore running plate, hoof-surface.

FIG. 126.

A fore running plate, ground-surface.

FIG. 127.

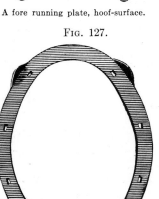

A hind running plate, hoof-surface.

FIG. 128.

A hind running plate, ground-surface.

Shoeing Trotters and Pacers.

The shoes worn while the trotter or pacer is in training are somewhat heavier than those worn while racing. Training shoes will average 40 ounces to the set, while trotting and pacing plates weigh from 16 to 28 ounces to the set. Of the six fastest trotters during the last year (1912) the average weight of the front shoes was 6⅝ ounces, of the hind shoes 4 ounces. Of the seven swiftest pacers of the same year the front shoes averaged 5½ ounces, and the hind shoes 3⅝ ounces. In short, *extreme speed at running, pacing or trotting demands as light a shoe as can be made, which will at the same time furnish a bearing for wall, white line and a narrow rim of the sole.*

In style of shoes there is no marked difference between trotters and pacers—except in the hind shoes of pacers that cross-fire (see cross-firing," p. 140). Open shoes predominate. Bar-shoes are used, not to give frog pressure, but to stiffen and prevent spreading of the shoe, when after a few days' wear it becomes thin at the toe. The average trotting and pacing plate is so thin that it would be weakened by fullering, so most of them are stamped (punched). Six nails are sufficient. Clips are seldom needed.

Pacers usually require a low circular grab or " rim " at the toe. This is set flush with the outer border, is about one-eighth of an inch high and is brazed on. Trotting plates are usually without toe calks, though many are fullered across the toe (corrugated) to furnish a grip upon the ground.

On both trotting and pacing shoes the heel calks should be low and sharp and should run straight forward so as not to retard the forward glide of the foot as it is set to earth heel first. The heel calk serves chiefly to prevent the lateral twist of the foot as the horse takes the sharp turns of the track.

Freak shoes, toe-weights, side-weights, excessive length of hoof or toe, and other unscientific appliances and methods of shoeing speed horses are being gradually eliminated, and to-day the fastest are dressed and shod in accordance with the principles enunciated in this book.

Fitting Shoes to Heavy Draft-Horses.

What has been previously said concerning shoeing holds good here; however, the conditions of shoeing are somewhat different in heavy horses, and particularly with respect to hoofs which, without being clearly diseased, have been injured by shoeing. The entire operation requires more circumspection, because it is more difficult. In many cases one will find that the width that has been advised for the outer branch of the shoe at the quarter is not sufficient. Indeed, if a horse has wry feet, and there is unequal distribution of weight within the hoof, and we attempt in shoeing it to follow to the letter the directions given on preceding pages, we would be apt to favor the perpetuation of the defect. In such cases the slant of the wall at the quarters is of the greatest practical value to us in estimating the proper width for the shoe at this point.

FIG. 129.

Left hind shoe with a broad, base-wide outer branch for draft-horses that stand markedly base-narrow (close behind).

When uniform setting down of the hoof and uniform wear of the shoe are desired, every point in the coronary band in the posterior half of the foot must receive support by the shoe. This applies particularly to the outer halves of hoofs that are extremely base-narrow. If, for example, the coronet of the outer quarter projects beyond the plantar border of the quarter, the outer branch of the shoe from the last nail-hole back must be kept so wide (full) that an imaginary perpendicular line dropped from the coronary band will just touch the outer border of the shoe. The inner branch, on the contrary, should follow the edge of the wall as closely as possible. Furthermore, the new shoe should be given more curve,—that is, made wider and fitted more full where the old shoe shows greatest wear. *The principal thought should be to set the shoe, which should always be regarded as the base of support of the hoof, farther towards the more strongly worn side.* Such a practice renders superfluous the wide-spread and popular custom of bending outward the outer quarter and heel-calk of hind shoes. From the manner in which a horse travels and the wear of the old shoe, we estimate the distance that the branches of the shoe should be set from the middle line of the hoof. If in following out this plan the bearing-surface of the outer quarter of the wall is not completely covered, the quarter will be pinched and squeezed inward; this should be prevented by a broader branch punched so deeply that the holes will fall upon the white line (Fig. 129).

When the shoer has satisfied himself that the shoe fulfils every requirement and fits perfectly, it is to be cooled, the holes opened with an oiled pritchel, and the shoe brightened with a file. In filing, all sharp edges should be removed. If a shoe is to be filed upon the outer border, to give it a neater appearance, the filing should be done *lengthways of the shoe,* and *not crossways;* of course, the shoe must not be bent by being improperly clamped in the vise.

It indicates much greater skill in making and fitting shoes when they look clean and finished with little or no filing.

In the preceding remarks I have insisted upon a horizontal bearing-surface for all shoes, with the single exception of shoes provided with the rolled toe (rolling motion). As far as I can judge from the literature of shoeing, and from what I have seen with my own eyes in many countries, this is the most wide-spread practice. In Germany, on the other hand, there is another method, followed in the military shoeing-shops, *which consists in placing the bearing-surface of the shoe as nearly as possible at right angles to the slant of the wall.* According to this method the bearing-surface of the shoe, depending upon the direction of the wall (viewed from in front, from behind, and from the side), should incline more or less, now backward, now inward, now horizontal, and now outward. Shoes for wide hoofs are given a bearing-surface which inclines inward, while for narrow hoofs the shoes have a horizontal bearing-surface. Shoes for wry hoofs have a bearing-surface which inclines downward and inward for the slanting wall, and for the steeper wall a horizontal bearing-surface, which towards the end of the branch may incline slightly downward and outward. Besides, the bearing-surface of the ends of the branches, viewed from the side, has a backward and downward inclination. This method is practicable **only in part.**

I. Nailing the Shoe.

This is that act of horseshoeing by which the shoe is fastened to the hoof by special nails called hoof-nails or horseshoe-nails, which are driven through the shoe and horny wall.

At present there are hand-made and machine-made horseshoe-nails. Both kinds should be made of the best wrought iron. The nails must be slender, wedge-shaped, and twice as wide as they are thick. Thickness and length must be in proper relation to each other. We should never choose a nail which is longer than is absolutely necessary to hold the shoe; six to eight sizes are sufficient for all purposes.

FIG. 130.

1.   2.   3.

Hand-made horseshoe-nails, natural size, for fullered shoes(1,not bevelled).

The rough nails (hand-made), before being used, must undergo a special shaping to prepare them to pass through the wall easily and in the desired direction. This preparation is called *shaping and bevelling.* In doing this we should see to it that the nails are made smooth, and even, but are not hammered harder than is absolutely necessary, because the lighter one can hammer the nails the better they will be.

Furthermore, we must give the nail that form which will insure its passing through the horn *straight* and *not in a curve;* with this object in view, the nail is to be slightly curved so that the side which is turned towards the frog in driving (inside) will be a little concave, the opposite side convex (Figs. 130, 3, and 131, No. 10), since it is known that a straight nail always passes through the horn in a curve, and not only does not long remain tight, but is quite likely to *press upon and injure the soft tissues* of the foot. (See, also, Nailing.)

At the point of the nail the *bevel* is to be so placed that it will form a short one-sided wedge with the slanting side

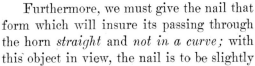

directed **from within to without** (Figs. 130, 3, and 131, *d*).
A short bevel is suitable for nails that are to be driven low,
while a long bevel makes it possible to drive them high. *The*
bevel should never form a hook; it must always be straight,
should be sharp but not thin, and under no conditions incom-
plete (defective).

FIG. 131.

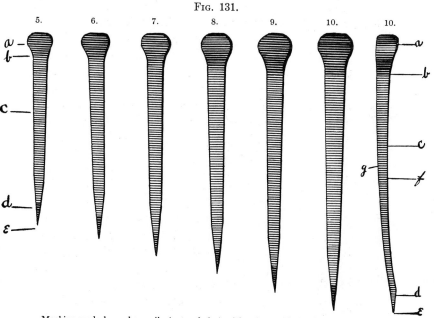

Machine-made horseshoe-nails (natural size) with a low, wide head for a fullered shoe.
The last nail is shown from one border; the others from the inner face: *a*, head; *b*, neck;
c, shank; *d*, bevel; *e*, point; *f*, inner face; *g*, outer face.

Machine-made nails, smooth, polished, bevelled, and ready
for use, are, for many reasons, to be preferred to hand-made
nails, though the latter are rather tougher (see Fig. 131).

Before the shoe is nailed on it should be cooled and again
carefully examined by a competent shoer, who should then
place it upon the hoof, where it should be critically observed to
see whether it really fulfils every requirement of a properly-

fitting shoe. Afterwards, the least fault or defect must be remedied, and then the work of *nailing* it begins. By nailing, the shoe is firmly and durably fastened to the hoof, in doing which the horn of the wall is spared so far as possible, the elasticity of the hoof borne always in mind, and wounding of the pododerm entirely avoided. **The nails must in all cases penetrate the white line** and pass through the wall in such a straight direction that they will appear neither too high nor too low upon its outer surface. In the first case there is considerable danger of pricking or close-nailing, and in the latter the nail-holes will tear out easily when the nails are being clinched.

FIG. 132.

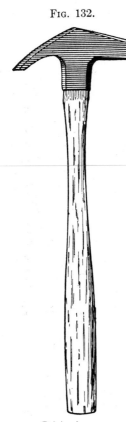

Driving hammer.

In driving a nail, it should be held in the fingers as long as possible in the direction in which it is desired that it shall pass through the horn. A nail should be driven cautiously, with attention to its *sinking and sound,* and yet with enough force so that at each stroke it will penetrate from one-fifth to one-fourth of an inch. The power required at each stroke will depend upon the hardness of the horn and the size of the nail. Fearless driving and timorous tapping should not be allowed.

Nails, which at a depth of five-eighths of an inch are still going soft, or which bend and give a dull sound, or cause pain, should be immediately withdrawn.

According to the size of the horse and his hoofs the nails should be driven from five-eighths to an inch and five-eighths high, and as *even* as possible. As soon as a nail is driven its point should be **immediately** bent down towards the shoe in order to prevent injuries. The heads of all the nails should then be gone over with a hammer and driven down solidly into the nail-holes, the hoof being meanwhile supported in the left hand. Pincers are then held under the bent nails and they are more sharply bent by *light* blows upon the nail-heads. The points of the nails are now nipped off near the hoof, the horn which has been thrown out just below the clinches by bending the nails down is removed with rasp or gouge, and the ends of the nails bent down still more, but not quite flush with the wall. This operation is called "clinching." A clinching-block or a pair of ordinary blacksmith's pincers is then placed under the end of the nail, now called a clinch, and by light blows (in doing this the nail must not bend within the wall) upon the head the clinch is turned closer to the surface of the wall; finally, with the front edge of the nail-hammer the clinch is hammered down flush with the wall. On the inner half of the wall the clinches should not be felt on stroking the wall with the fingers. The small amount of horn that projects beyond the shoe around the toe may be carefully rasped away in the direction in which the wall slants, but *never higher than the clinches;* finally, the sharp lower edge of the wall is to be removed by carrying the corner of the rasp around between the shoe and the horn.

A clinch is sufficiently long when it equals the width of the nail at that point.

It is of advantage to use a shoeing-bock or foot-stool in clinching the nails on the front hoofs. The hind hoofs may be clinched in the hands. Then the horse should be led out and again moved in order to see whether or not the new shoeing has actually accomplished what was desired. Finally, the entire hoof should be given a thin layer of hoof-salve.

K. Horseshoes More or Less Deficient in the Desirable Qualities Described on Pages 107-116.

Machine Shoes.

1. *Machine Shoes of Wrought Iron.*—They are half-finished and finished. Though machine shoes with few exceptions show no distinction between front and hind, or left and right, with correct punching for these different feet, but usually present one form in different sizes, yet, unfortunately, they are in high favor with horseshoers, because they may be used for both summer and winter and for bar shoes.

FIG. 133.   FIG. 134.

A machine-made (drop-forged) front shoe, ground surface.

A machine-made toe-weight front shoe for a harness horse, showing ground surface. Punching good.

For these reasons we cannot approve of machine shoes.

2. *Finished Cast Shoes.*—They are of four kinds,—ordinary cast shoes, cast shoes with rope buffer, cast shoes with fiber buffer, and cast shoes fenestrated to hold a rubber buffer. Ordinary cast shoes of correct form and proper punching designed by Grossbauer, of Vienna, are sold by Hannes' Sons, of that city.

Rope Shoes.—These shoes have a groove on the ground surface, in which rests a tarred rope, which greatly diminishes
slipping on smooth pavement. For this reason alone they are

FIG. 135.   FIG. 136.   FIG. 137.

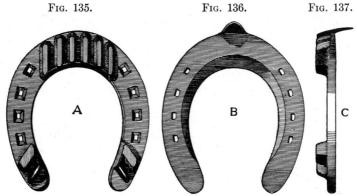

Machine-made (drop-forged) multi-calk fore shoe. *A*, ground-surface; *B*, hoof-surface
C, profile.

FIG. 138.   FIG. 139.   FIG. 140.

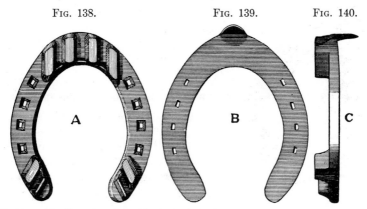

Machine-made (drop forged) multi-calk hind shoe. *A*, ground-surface; *B*, hoof-surface;
C, profile.

extensively used in the large cities of Germany. Since the open
rope shoe, when half worn out, will warp, the bar rope shoe is
more satisfactory and more extensively used (Figs. 141–144).

Before fitting the shoe the rope must be removed. After the nails are driven it is laid in the groove and hammered into

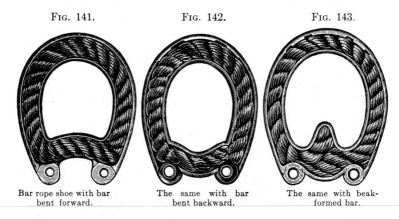

Fig. 141.	Fig. 142.	Fig. 143.
Bar rope shoe with bar bent forward.	The same with bar bent backward.	The same with beak-formed bar.

place. Rope shoes can seldom be fitted properly to hoofs other than those which are healthy and of regular shape.

Fig. 144.

An open rope shoe.

Fiber Shoes.—These have a groove on the ground surface into which layers of linen fiber belting have been tightly pressed. The fiber cannot be removed, and therefore the shoes cannot be heated, but must be fitted cold. The nail-holes are placed between the fiber and the outer border of the shoe, and are punched too light. The bearing surface of the shoe is unsupported, so that when the shoe is half worn out, it warps. There is no distinction between rights and lefts.

Rubber shoes have all the defects of fiber shoes, and one more. The hoof surface is covered with canvas, which under normal and acute-angled hoofs wears through under the quarters and leads to loosening of the last nails.

L. Rubber Pads.

The increasing use of asphalt, tarvia and other hard, smooth and slippery materials for surfacing city streets and country highways has not only made travelling in flat and even in calked shoes precarious, but has aggravated all those injuries produced by concussion.

To prevent slipping and the injurious effects of concussion a great many shoes have been devised, in which are incorporated such materials as hemp rope, linen fibre, papier maché, cork, wood, bast, felt and rubber, but all fail in greater or lesser degree to meet practical requirements.

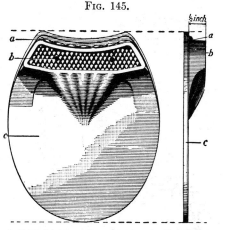

FIG. 145.

A light driving pad, gummed and stitched to a leather sole; seen from the ground surface and in profile. Used with a seven- to ten-ounce short shoe. *a*, stitching; *b*, rubber bar under buttress and frog; *c*, leather sole.

Rubber, though the most expensive of these materials, is the most resilient and takes the best grip on smooth pavement. A pad of rubber, wide enough to cover the branches of the frog alone, or the branches of the frog and the buttresses of the hoof, firmly cemented to a leather sole, constitutes the modern rubber pad (Figs. 145, 146, 147).

The frog-and-buttress pad used with a short shoe is to be preferred to the earlier frog pad which takes a full shoe.

The advantages of rubber pads are:

1. They prevent slipping upon asphalt and other smooth, dry surfaces.

2. They diminish concussion, and are valuable in the

prevention and treatment of sore heels, dry and moist corns, bruised sole, and incipient side bone.

3. They give frog pressure, develop the frog and tend to prevent contraction of the quarters and those lesions which may follow contraction, as corns, cracks of bars and quarters, laminitis of the quarters and thrush.

A rubber pad should not be used:

1. In contraction of one or both quarters, when the frog is too much shrunken to bear upon the pad.

Fig. 146.   Fig. 147.

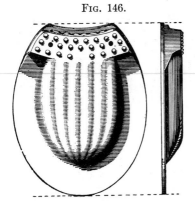   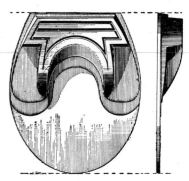

Air-cushion pad, seen from ground surface and in profile. Suitable for light harness horses.

A heavy bar-pad suitable for heavy harness and draft-horses on pavement. The short shoe may carry a toe-calk of medium height.

2. In lameness from well developed side bones.

3. In navicular bursitis (" navicular disease ").

4. In thrush, or canker of frog or sole.

Rubber pads, light, medium and heavy, are made in all sizes and are suitable for all classes of horses, from the light roadster to the heavy draft type. The short shoe with which they are used reaches the middle of the quarters. The pad surface (upper surface) of the ends of the branches should be bevelled to conform to the pad, and to hold it firmly against the frog and buttresses.   The thickness of the shoe should equal two-thirds the thickness of the pad, so that when fitted one-third of the thickness of the pad shall project below the ground-surface of the shoe.   The shoe should be provided with a strong toe-clip.   With the heavy, thick pad of a draft-horse a low toe-calk may be used, but heel calks should never be put on a short shoe.   Pads are seldom necessary on the hind feet.

CHAPTER IV.

SHOEING HORSES THAT FORGE AND INTERFERE.

A. Forging.

FORGING is that defect of the horse's gait by reason of which, at a trot, he strikes the ends of the branches or the under surface of the front shoe with the toe of the hind shoe or hoof of the same side. Forging in a pacer is termed " cross-firing " and consists in striking the inner quarter, or the under surface of the inner branch of a front shoe with the toe of the diagonal hind shoe or hoof.

Forging is unpleasant to hear and dangerous to the horse. It is liable to wound the heels of the forefeet, damages the toes or the coronet of the hind hoofs, and often pulls off the front shoes.

FIG. 148.

Right front shoe with concave ground-surface ("convex iron") to prevent "forging."

FIG. 149.

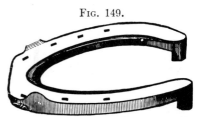

Right hind shoe with lateral toe-clips to prevent "clicking" and the various injuries due to forging.

Causes.—1. Faulty conformation; for example, horses that stand considerably higher ·at the croup than at the withers; horses with long legs and short bodies; horses that " stand under " in front and behind. 2. Using horses on heavy ground, unskilful driving, allowing a long-necked, heavy-headed horse

138

to carry his head too low; riding without holding a horse to his work by feeling his mouth and pressing the knees against his sides. 3. Fatigue frequently leads to forging, even in horses that are well built and properly shod. It may also occur in the act of vaulting over an obstacle. 4. Poor shoeing, especially too long toes upon the front and hind hoofs, and too long front shoes.

The aim of the shoer should be to facilitate the quick and easy " breaking over " of the **front foot,** so that it may get away before it is overtaken by the hind foot. The toe of the front hoof should be fairly short and rolled ; the quarters spared. The front shoe should be light, rolled at the toe and **no longer and no wider** than the hoof. The ends of the branches of a flat shoe, and also the heel-calks, in case they are needed to elevate a heel that is too low, should be bevelled from the hoof surface of the shoe downward and forward under the foot. Such short heel-calks, bevelled to prevent forging, are called " forging calks." If the horse continues to forge between the branches and against the ground surface of the shoe, concaving this surface will prove advantageous (convex iron). The form of the front shoes of horses that forge should represent merely a prolongation of the hoof.

The " breaking over " of the **hind foot** should be delayed by sparing the toe and lowering the quarters, but not sufficiently to break the foot-axis too far backward. The hind shoe is to be squared at the toe and the lower edge of the shoe in the region of the toe well rounded; instead of a toe-clip, two side-clips are to be drawn up and the shoe so fitted that at least three-fourths of the thickness of the wall of the toe, with the edge well rounded, will extend forward beyond the shoe. Should the toe of the hoof be short it may be raised either by a low toe-calk set one-fourth of an inch back from the edge of the shoe, or by thinning the shoe from the toe to the ends of the branches. The branches of a flat hind shoe should extend somewhat farther back of the buttresses than under normal conditions, to trail upon the ground just before the hoof alights, and acting as a brake, to bring the hoof to earth (Fig. 150).

" Cross-firing " is most apt to occur and is most dangerous at extreme speed.   Then, when the inner branch of the hind shoe strikes the inner heel, quarter or shoe of the diagonal front foot, both feet are in the air,—the fore foot is approaching the middle of its stride, while the offending hind foot is in the last third of its flight.   The standing position that favors cross-firing is the base-wide (toe-wide) in front, and the base-narrow (toe-narrow) behind.   With this direction of limbs the

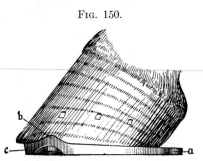

FIG. 150.

flight of the fore feet is forward and inward during the first half of their stride, while the flight of the hind feet is forward and inward during the second half of their stride (see Figs. 72, 73, 75).

The problem is, therefore, so to pare and shoe a base-wide fore foot that it will break over nearer the centre of the toe and thus execute less of an inward swing during the first half

Hind shoe with swelled toe to slow the breaking over.   Often efficient when the hoof is too short at the toe: a, long branches to trail and bring the foot to earth; b, outer-toe clip; c, toe squared and set under to prevent injury to front hoof, and to deaden the sound of forging.

of its stride, and to so pare and shoe a base-narrow hind foot that it will break over nearer the centre of the toe and thus execute less of an inward swing during the second half of its stride.   Neither a toe-wide nor a toe-narrow foot can be made to break over the exact centre of the toe, and yet it is possible by dressing the hoof and by shoeing to shift the breaking over point nearer to the centre of the toe, and by doing so, to alter slightly the lines of flight of the feet.

Dressing and shoeing the front foot: **The hoof** should be relatively low from the middle of the toe around to and including the *outer* buttress. If the inner half of the wall is deficient in length it must be raised above the outer half by applying a shoe which is thinner in its outer than in its inner branch. The inner toe should be left long.

The shoe should be light, without heel-calks, but may carry a low, curved grab ("grab," is a low, straight or curved,

FIG. 151.

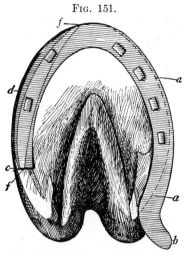

FIG. 152.

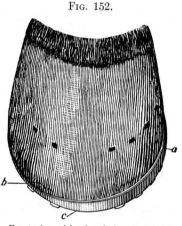

Left hind hoof of a toe-narrow pacer, shod to prevent crossfiring: *a*, dotted line indicating outer border of the hoof; *b*, long bent outer branch; *c*, short, thin inner branch; *d*, inner wall extending beyond the shoe; *f*, line from which inner branch is feather-edged. The shoe is of even thickness from *b* to *f* at inner toe; but from latter point to *c* diminishes to a feather edge.

Front view of hoof and shoe depicted in Fig. 151: *a*, outer branch fitted very full and bevelled base wide; *b*, inner branch diminishing in thickness from inner toe *c*, to its termination at the inner quarter. Designed to favor "breaking over" near centre of the toe, and to widen the gait.

toe- or heel-calk on a racing plate) running from the second inner toe nail to the centre of the toe. *The inner branch* is to be fitted flush with the wall from the centre of the toe back to the quarter, back of which point it gradually extends beyond the wall, *i.e.,* is fitted full; and terminates well back of the buttress. *This inner branch* should be from one-fourth to three-eighths of an inch longer than the outer branch. *The long inner branch, full at the quarter, is desirable, but must be covered by a quarter-boot, which a cross-firer should always wear.*

The outer branch should be fitted snug and terminate at the buttress. From the centre of the toe to the end of the branch the ground surface should be bevelled from the inner edge of the web to a knife-edge at the outer border.

Dressing and shoeing the hind foot: **The hoof** should be relatively low from the centre of the toe around to and including the *inner* buttress. If the outer half of the hoof is deficient in length, it must be raised above the inner half by applying a shoe with a thin inner branch. The inner branch may terminate in a knife-edge midway between toe and heel (Figs. 151 and 152).

The inner branch is to be fitted snug from the centre of the toe to its end, and its ground surface should be bevelled from the inner edge of the web to a knife-edge at the outer border.

The outer branch is to be fitted very full from the outside toe to the end. This branch should extend well behind the buttress, and in well-marked base-narrow hoofs should be turned outward in order to support the overhanging coronet of the quarter. The outer border should be bevelled base-wide, and the nail holes punched coarse, *i.e.*, far in from the outer border (Figs. 151 and 152). The outer branch may carry a small heel-calk.

B. Interfering.

A horse "interferes" when a hoof in motion strikes the opposite supporting leg. Interfering is apt to produce injuries, either of the coronary band of the inner half of the foot or of the fetlock-joint, or (in fore-limbs) of the cannon, even as high up as the knee. Lameness frequently accompanies such injuries.

The causes of interfering lie either in the *shoeing* (of the

foot that strikes, as well as of the foot which is struck), in
the *position of the limbs,* or in the *use* of the animal. Horses
that have the correct standing position do not interfere when
they are properly shod; base-wide horses interfere sometimes;
horses base-narrow down to the fetlock and toe-wide below that
point interfere very frequently. Traces of unequal length,
weariness, and shoeing at too long intervals favor interfering.

In attempting to lessen or remove interfering, the horse
must be most carefully examined with respect to the position
of his limbs, his gait, and his
shoeing, in the manner described on pages 90 to 92.

If the cause is found to be
the twisted position of a shoe,
too wide hoofs, raised clinches,
etc., nothing need be done further than to correct the shoeing;
but if a faulty position of the
limbs is the cause, we must
ascertain the exact part of the
hoof that does the striking,
diminish the size of the hoof
at that point, regulate the entire plantar surface of the hoof,
make the shoe straight along
the region that strikes,—that is,

Fig. 153.

A right front shoe with nailless and
narrow inner branch for a base-wide hoof.
Suitable for horses that strike anywhere
from inner toe back to the quarter.

without curve,—and so fit it to the foot that one-third of the
thickness of the wall will extend beyond the shoe. Where interfering is so pronounced as to produce serious injuries, we
use a shoe with no nails in the inner branch (" dropped-crease "
shoe) (Figs. 153, 156, 157).

The so-called *interfering shoes* (Figs. 154 and 155) are
worthy of recommendation only for hoofs of the base-narrow
position. The interfering branch, whose greater thickness
raises the inner wall, which is often too low, is to be so shaped

and directed that the hoof will project somewhat beyond it. *This interfering branch must be made and shaped in accordance with each individual case.* The holes in the interfering

FIG. 154.

Left hind shoe with interfering branch (ground surface), for base-narrow standing position.

FIG. 155.

The same (hoof-surface).

FIG. 156.

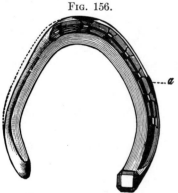

Left hind interfering shoe without nail-holes in inner branch ("dropped-crease" shoe): a, side-clip.

FIG. 157.

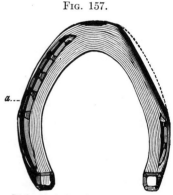

Right hind shoe for toe-cutters. The dotted lines indicate the distance that the wall projects beyond the shoe: a, side-clip.

branch should be punched somewhat finer (nearer the edge) than usual. Interfering shoes in which the nail-holes, with the exception of the inner toe nail-hole, are placed in the outer branch, are called " *dropped-crease interfering shoes* " (Fig. 156). Such shoes are not recommended for hind hoofs that are decidedly toe-wide (toe-cutters); in such cases better results will be obtained by using a shoe, either with or without heel-calks, whose inner branch is straight and without nails along the striking region, and is fitted wide (full) at the quarter. The inner branch should be from one-fourth to three-eighths of an inch longer than the outer. The inner heel-calk should be higher than the outer, and the end of the outer branch should be as base-narrow as it can be made (fitted close) (Fig. 157). In order to prevent shifting of an interfering shoe, a side-clip should be drawn up on the outer branch (*a*).

There is no manner of shoeing that will prevent interfering which is caused by improper harnessing, crooked hitching, or weariness. The simpler and the *lighter* the shoes the less will horses interfere.

CHAPTER V.

WINTER SHOEING.

ALL shoes whose ground-surface is provided with contrivances to prevent slipping upon snow and ice are called winter shoes.

These various contrivances are produced by several processes called "methods of sharpening." All methods may be gathered into two groups,—namely, *practical* sharp-shoeing and *impractical*. Only the first will be considered.

FIG. 158.

The durability of sharpened shoes depends partly upon whether they are made of steel or iron, and partly upon the nature of the ground in winter. If the ground is continuously covered with a thick layer of snow, whatever method of sharpening is followed, the shoes **stay sharp**; if, however, the winter is open, changeable, with more bare ice than snow, no method of sharpening, whatever it may be, will last long; the shoes will **not stay sharp**.

For these reasons no method of sharpening which fulfils all conditions satisfactorily has yet been discovered.

An ice-nail, frost-nail.

The simplest and at the same time the least durable method of sharpening is: 1. That by means of **ice-nails** or **frost-nails** (Fig. 158). One or two nails are drawn from each branch of the shoe and replaced with ice-nails.

2. **Sharp Toe- and Heel-Calks.**—The outer calk is split and a small steel wedge welded in. It is then laid upon the edge of the anvil, indented and sharpened from within to without in such a manner that the calk shall be thin from

146

the branch to the ground, and the outer surface shall be in the same vertical plane as the outer edge. If a calk is narrow from its base to its end, and at the same time without flaw, it does not need a sharp cutting edge. The inner calk should never be sharpened except the ground be very slippery. The cutting edge of this inner calk stands at right angles to the length of the branch, and its outer corner should then be rounded to prevent its injuring the opposite foot (Figs. 159, 160).

Fig. 159.   Fig. 160.

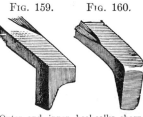

Outer and inner heel-calks sharpened.

For horses used for heavy draft purposes a toe-calk is welded to the shoe and sharpened. For this purpose we use only steel (toe-steel), which is easily welded to the shoe and remains firm. Toe-calks and steeled heel-calks are tempered, in order, as much as possible, to lengthen their period of durability. This method of sharpening is the oldest and most wide - spread, and is employed on the shoes of all horses of which we require more than light service.

Fig. 161.

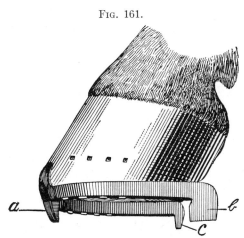

Left fore hoof sharp shod: *a*, toe-calk bevelled from in front; *b*, outer heel-calk directed lengthwise with the branch; *c*, inner heel-calk, half sharp and directed transversely to direction of the branch.

Hoofs are easily damaged or even ruined by frequently repeated sharpening of the shoes, because every time this is done the shoes must be removed and replaced.

3. **Shoeing with Screw Heel-Calks.**—Any ordinary flat shoe not too thin and narrow at the ends of the branches can be changed to a shoe with screw heel-calks by punching holes in the ends of the branches and cutting a thread in them.

The screw heel-calk holes are made either by punching or boring. The punching is done by means of an almost cylindrical hammer-punch, afterwards finishing the holes by driving through them a round punch which tapers from the middle towards both ends. On the ground-surface of the shoe the hole is moderately counter-sunk (Fig. 162, *a*), so that after the thread has been cut and the calk screwed into place the shoulder of the latter will rest on the counter-sinking.

Fig. 162.

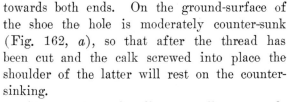

At present nearly all screw-calks are made by machinery, either of iron or toe-steel. The former is too soft and therefore not sufficiently durable; the latter, however, is quite durable when the calk is properly hardened (tempered) by heating to a cherry-red, sticking the head of the calk as far as the tap into a bed of moist sand, and allowing it to slowly cool.

Ground-surface of the end of a branch of shoe, showing (*a*) hole and counter-sinking for a screw-calk (one-half natural size).

The chief requirements of a good screw-calk are, further, a **clean, deep,** but not too coarse **thread,** and but *one size of thread and tap for all calks,* so that every calk will fit in every shoe. A calk whose tap measures one-half inch (12.7 millimetres) (Whitworth) in diameter is sufficient for the heaviest shoes. The tap which is used to cut the thread in the holes for the screw-calks must be about $\frac{1}{125}$ of an inch thicker than the head of the calk. In the German army the calks have a tap fifteen thirty-seconds of an inch in diameter. The coachman should be given four calks (sharp and blunt) for each shoe, and a small screw-calk key for placing and removing them. Screw toe-calks are also used, yet they require special security to prevent their becoming loose. Experimentation with the screw toe-calks, though not yet entirely satisfactory, cannot be said to have ended.

The advantages of shoes provided with good screw heel-calks are so manifold that they deserve marked preference over shoes sharpened by the ordinary methods. The common objections urged against screw-calks,—namely, that they loosen and are lost, or break off, are not worthy of serious consideration, since these evils are merely the result of unskilful workmanship and poor ma-

Fig. 164.

Fig. 163.

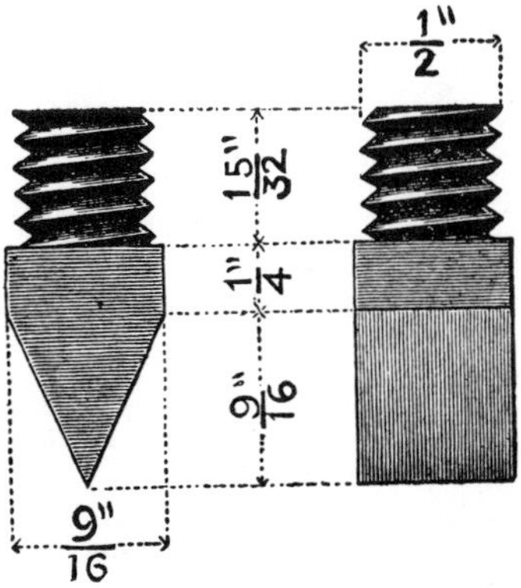

Sharp screw-calks with Whitworth thread
(half-inch, natural size).

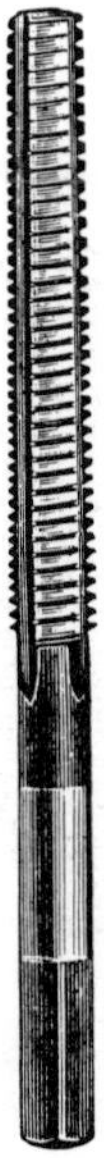

Whitworth tap (half-inch,
half natural size).

terial. *Shoes with screw heel-calks are the best shoes for winter, especially for horses that have to work hard and continuously.*

Balling with snow is prevented by using shoes narrow in the web and concave upon the ground-surface (convex iron), and thoroughly oiling the sole and frog. Sole-pads of felt, leather, or straw serve the same purpose. Balling with snow is *best* prevented by a rubber sole-and-frog pad, or by a " stopping " of a patent hoof cement known in Germany as "huflederkitt."

4. Shoeing with Peg-Calks.—The calks are merely stuck into the calk-holes, hence their name. Round and square peg-calks are used, but the former are better than the latter.

The inventor of round peg-calks is Judson, an American. The shoes differ in no respect from the ordinary flat shoes. It is necessary that the tap of the calk have a moderately conical form, and exactly fit into the calk-hole of the shoe. The taper of the calk-tap is correct if for every ten thirty-seconds of an inch in length it increases or diminishes one-thirty-second of an inch in diameter (equal to one inch in every ten inches of length).

Although the calk-holes may be punched in a hot shoe, yet boring and reaming them is much better, because by this method a more perfect fit can be secured. For this purpose we require a drill (a spiral drill is the best) whose diameter is exactly the same as that of the small end of the calk-tap (Figs. 165, *c,* and 166, *c*). After the shoe has been fitted to the hoof, the provisional holes are drilled and afterwards reamed out from the ground-surface of the shoe with the reamer shown in Fig. 167. Since the tap of the reamer corresponds exactly in size to the tap of the calk, it is evident that the latter must exactly fit and be tight. The wire edge that is raised around the hole is removed with a file, and the edge then smoothed by introducing the reamer a second time. The calks are made of rolled round steel, which has the thickness of the tap-end of the calk. For this purpose we require a calk-mould or matrix, in which one or more holes have been finished with a reamer. A piece of rod steel is heated at the end for a distance nearly twice the length of the calk, is swaged, thrust into the matrix, then broken off, and backset. This will give a blunt peg-calk. If a sharp calk is desired, the upper part of the head of the calk is sharpened in the ordinary manner, although this is accomplished most easily by using a pair of tongs with short jaws that are hollowed upon the inside for seizing the tap of the calk.

Fig. 165.   Fig. 166.   Fig. 167.

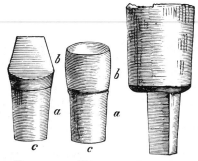

Sharp peg-calk (cog): *a,* the tap; *b,* the head.   Blunt peg-calk: *a,* the tap; *b,* the head   Lower part of the reamer.

Before the shoes are nailed on, the normal punch should be oiled and driven into the calk-holes, and the calks passed into the holes to see that they fit perfectly.

The calks are driven into place **after** the shoes are nailed to the hoofs. A light blow is sufficient to fasten a calk, yet a necessary precaution is first to remove every trace of oil from the calks and calk-holes. The first calk driven into place must be held with the hand while the second is being driven, otherwise it will either spring from the calk-hole or be loosened so that it will soon afterwards be lost.

To remove such a calk we strike its head from different sides with a hammer, stone, or other hard object until it becomes loose, when a rather hard blow upon the shoe causes it to spring out. Calks which have worn down are seized by a pair of sharp nippers and loosened by blows upon the shoe. Since a calk which is firm soon rusts and is then very difficult to remove, it is recommended that all calks be removed every night.

The **advantages** of peg-calks over screw-calks are: 1. They do not break off. 2. They are easier to make and simpler to use. 3. They are **cheaper.**

Disadvantages.—1. Peg-calks are sometimes lost, even when properly made and most carefully introduced. This evil happens much less frequently when the calks are put in by the maker (horseshoer) than when they are stuck in by the coachman, attendant, rider, or other person. When calks are lost on the way from the shop, it is usually due to some fault in the calk-holes or in the calks, although when the feet are balled with snow the calks are easily lost, because they do not then touch the ground.

2. The removal of the calks often involves many difficulties, since they are apt to rust into place if not removed daily, and when worn down so far that they cannot be grasped with the pincers are almost impossible to remove. By hammering upon the calks and shoe many horses are rendered not only restive, but sensitive in the feet.

3. If horses are used without the calks, a wire-edge forms around the hole on the bottom of the shoe, which interferes with the placing of the calk and lessens its security.

The **hollow peg-calk** (Fig. 168), made by Branscheid & Philippi, of Remscheid, has considerable merit. It holds exceedingly well, and is very durable. It is furnished in three sizes,—Nos. 12, 13, and 14,—of twenty-seven, thirty-one, and thirty-four millimetres length, and twelve, thirteen, and fourteen millimetres diameter at the end of the tap.

A punch is furnished which, when driven up to its head in the holes of the heated shoe, insures a proper width and shape of the hole and an accurately fitting calk.

The calks may be removed by an extractor (Fig. 169) having at one end a thread which is screwed into a corresponding thread on the inside of the hollow calk, when by a few hammer blows on the shoe the calk loosens. To prevent the calk becoming choked with dirt, a piece of cork is thrust into the hollow. It may be easily removed by means of the corkscrew at the other end of the extractor.

5. **Shoeing with Peg Toe-Calks.**—These are an invention of considerable worth, especially for heavy draft in hilly country. They render better service on hind than on front shoes.

Peg toe-calks with a single tap are simpler and preferable to those with two

Fig. 168.

Hollow - spring peg - calk, No. 12.

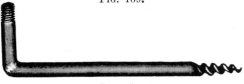

Fig. 169.

Peg-puller.

taps. Every known contrivance to prevent the occasional loss of the peg toe-calk is impractical.

The shoe for a peg toe-calk should be of good tough material and without a flaw. The toe of the shoe should be about one-twelfth to one-tenth of an inch thicker than the branches.

The hole for the peg toe-calk, whatsoever its shape may be, must be smooth and uniform, with clean, true corners. Semi-circular holes should present the convex side towards the toe.

Before punching, draw up the toe-clip. A punch-plate with a good-sized hole, and a tap which will fit into the square hole in the anvil will facilitate the work. The punch-plate when in position should be flush with the front edge of the anvil. Place the toe of the shoe, hoof surface upward, over the hole of the punch-plate, and drive a hole with a punch-hammer which is perceptibly thinner than the model punch. Now turn the shoe over, punch back from the ground surface, and then file away the wire edge which the punch has raised on the ground surface. Next, take a hand-punch, the end of which should just enter the hole, punch through from the ground surface, and correct any bulging by dressing lightly over the horn of the anvil. Finally, use the model punch to give the hole the exact size and smoothness.

Should the hole in the toe of the shoe enlarge in time, as sometimes occurs, then backset when necessary on removing the shoe. Backsetting is easiest with the half-round hole, because

Fig. 170.

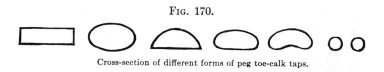

Cross-section of different forms of peg toe-calk taps.

the curved side, being turned forward, runs approximately parallel to the outer border of the toe of the shoe.

A good serviceable peg toe-calk must possess the following characteristics:

1. The tap must be of such shape as not to turn; therefore, not round.

2. The tap must be cone-shaped, and diminish in diameter about one-thirty-second of an inch for each one-fourth of an inch of its length from base to apex. If the tap has less taper it will enlarge the hole in the shoe till the head of the calk comes into contact with the shoe, when the calk will loosen and drop out.

3. The tap must be full-formed and smooth.

4. It must fit air-tight in the toe, and a single hammer-blow should be sufficient to fix it securely.

5. The **head** of the toe-calk **must not rest on the shoe;**
a space of one-sixteenth of an inch should intervene.

While a shoer of average mechanical ability can make a
faultless peg toe-calk, it is not profitable to do so while good
machine-made calks are to be had very cheap.

FIG. 171.

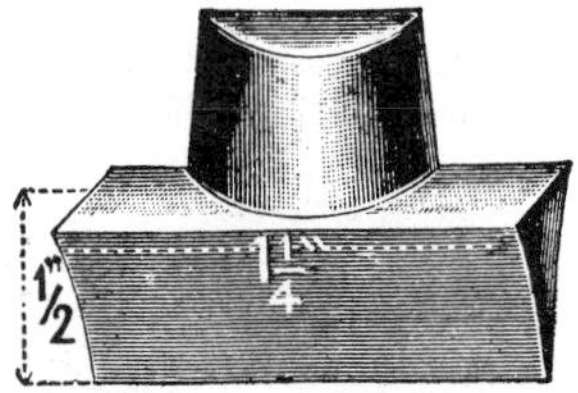

FIG. 172.

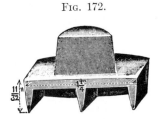

Chisel toe-calk. (Doring.) No. 1 from
the firm of Branscheid & Philippi, of Remscheid.

Shovel toe-calk.

FIG. 173.

FIG. 174.

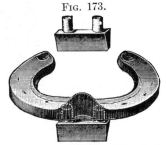

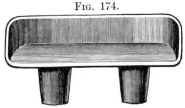

Peg toe-calk shoeing after Fisher-Renker,
of Dresden.

Peg-calk (shovel-calk) after Kunze-Klotzs-
che-Königswald, of Dresden.

The best forms in use are the quadrangular heads, with
oval, half-round (Figs. 171 and 172), and with two taps (Figs.
173 and 174).

In several European countries the peg toe-calks with half-
round tap and with two round taps are in use. To make good
peg toe-calk shoes and fit the calks properly requires **more
than ordinary knowledge and skill.** Poor work does much
harm. Therefore, work carefully and get well paid for it.

6. **Removable Heel-Calks that do not Require Sharpening.**
—The undeniable fact that all chisel-shaped or pyramid-shaped

sharp calks become dull in time, and must then either be sharpened or replaced by new calks, renders shoeing not only costly, but injurious to the hoofs and annoying to the owner. This drawback is most pronounced in large cities, where the snow never lies long upon the streets, and the horse just sharp-shod is soon obliged to travel upon bare pavements. Attempts have been made to lessen this annoyance by the use of calks that do *not require sharpening,* and yet which will prevent

FIG. 175.

Screw-calk with H-formed cross-section.

FIG. 176.

Screw-calk with +-formed cross-section.

slipping even after they have been used for a long time upon bare pavements. It cannot be denied that such calks have considerable value, and, except when the ground is covered with ice, many of these calks render excellent service. Just as the ordinary sharp calks are satisfactory and very durable outside of the large cities, so now for the first time a few of these recently invented sharp calks seem to be worthy of recommendation for city use. The following are the best:

1. Screw-calks and peg-calks with H-shaped cross-section (Fig. 175).

2. Screw-calks with +-shaped cross-section (Fig. 176).

3. Screw- and peg-calks with O-shaped cross-section (Fig. 176).

4. Screw- and peg-calks with S-shaped cross-section.

5. Angle-calks (Fig. 177).

6. Screw- and peg-calks with rubber foot-pad.

7. Screw-calks with Y star-shaped cross-section (Fig. 178).

8. Hollow wedge-calks (Fig. 179).

9. Perforated screw-calks (Fig. 180).

There is no doubt that the grip that these calks take upon the ground and their durability depend upon the diameter and the arrangement of their surfaces of friction. From all ex-

FIG. 177.	FIG. 178.	FIG. 179.	FIG. 180.

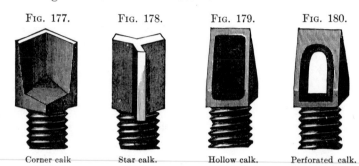

Corner calk.	Star calk.	Hollow calk.	Perforated calk.

FIG. 181.

Universal screw-calk key with tap.

FIG. 182.

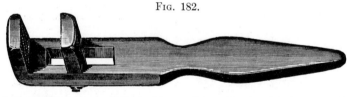

Felber's hand-vise to secure the hoof from twisting while changing the screw-calks.

periments made thus far it is shown that those calks which have narrow and comparatively few surfaces of friction are the least durable.

To introduce and remove the calks we use a calk key or wrench. For the shop, the ordinary fork key (Fig. 181), the jaws of which are tempered, is recommended. It fits all calks.

CHAPTER VI.

HOOF NURTURE.

Hoof nurture comprises all those measures which are employed to keep hoofs healthy, elastic, and serviceable.

A. Care of Unshod Hoofs.

The care of the hoofs of colts is of special importance. *Abundant exercise* upon dry ground which is not too stony is most beneficial. Such exercise will cause the hoofs to wear gradually, and it will only be necessary from time to time to observe whether the wear is taking place uniformly, and if not, to correct the uneven wear with the rasp.

Fig. 183.

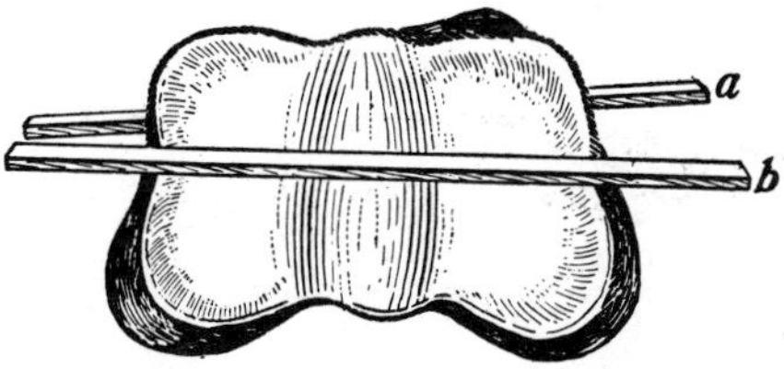

Twisted left front long pastern of colt, viewed from the upper articular surface. The lower end has been twisted toward the left: *a*, transverse axis of lower articular surface; *b*, transverse axis of the upper articular surface.

If colts are reared in the stable, the horn continuing to grow down does not undergo sufficient wear, and changes in form of the hoof, and even permanent distortions of the bones of the foot gradually occur. The wall becomes too long and bends or sometimes separates from the sole and keraphyllous layer. Weak quarters bend (curl) inward and encroach upon the space occupied by the frog (contracted feet of colts). The toe becomes too long, and this gives rise to too steep a position of the pastern and causes an insecure and diffident gait; therefore the hoofs must be shortened from time to time. The incurved quarters should be removed with the hoof-knife, and the outer edge of the plantar border of the wall well rounded with the rasp. In the base-wide and base-narrow standing positions the outer and inner walls respectively become relatively long and induce the colt to assume a still more abnormal position. The young and pliant pasterns may thus become permanently twisted and distorted (see Figs. 183 and 184). In a hoof that is becoming awry, restoring to the wall its proper level with relation to the

Fig. 184.

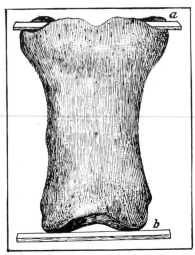

Left front long pastern of a colt showing compression shortening of outer half: *a*, transverse axis of upper articulation; *b*, transverse axis of coronary joint, not parallel to upper axis.

position of the limb will not only be invaluable in ultimately producing a good hoof, but will improve the faulty position of the limb. In exceptional cases, where the plantar border of some section of the wall gives evidence of too rapid wear, the application of a tip or of a half-shoe may be of benefit. Furthermore, we should attempt to secure greater cleanliness by frequently and thoroughly washing the hoofs and bedding with plenty of good straw.

Too early shoeing of young horses is very injurious; it hinders the development of the hoofs, and, furthermore, young horses when shod are frequently seriously overworked and prematurely ruined. Moderate work in the fields does not injure young horses, but for such service they do not require shoes.

The unshod hoofs of older horses should be periodically rounded with a rasp and the length of the walls regulated when, by reason of a lack of exercise, proper wear has not taken place.

B. Care of Shod Hoofs.

Shod hoofs are exposed to many more injuries than are unshod hoofs, because shoeing itself, although absolutely necessary to render horses continuously serviceable upon hard streets, is injurious to the hoof, since it to a greater or less extent prevents the physiological movements of the different parts of the foot, interferes with the circulation of the blood in the foot, slows the growth of the horn, and brings about a gradual shrinking of the entire hoof.

In addition, there are the injurious consequences of stabulation. These are *prevention of free movement, uncleanliness* due to bad floors and filthy bedding,—as, for example, peat moss and soiled straw,—and *dryness.*

Continuous standing always contributes to contraction of the hoofs, and this evil is greatly favored by dryness, which more particularly affects the front hoofs. The hind hoofs receive sufficient moisture from the animal's manure. Poor floors, particularly those that are uneven, tire the limbs. Accumulation of manure and the *careless* use of stationary sole-pads induce thrush of the frog.

The object of hoof nurture is to lessen or entirely remove all these injurious consequences of shoeing and stabulation. It comprises, therefore, not only the proper shortening of the hoofs every five to six weeks, but careful attention to *cleanliness and moisture.* Both are insured by dry straw and daily picking out and washing the hoofs. Such measures will prevent thrush in the hind feet. If front hoofs are washed once a day, sufficient moisture will penetrate the horn to give it that degree of suppleness (elasticity) which is possessed by an unshod hoof, and which contributes to a proper expansion of the hoof when the body-weight is placed upon it. *In order to prevent a hoof from again drying out,* the entire hoof should receive a thorough application of an oil or ointment (hoof-salve). *The object of greasing the horn is to prevent evaporation of the moisture that has penetrated the horn.* Specially compounded hoof-salves are not necessary. Melted horse-grease, pork-fat, or any other fat that is not rancid is sufficient. Cosmoline is an excellent hoof-salve.

Abundant but not excessive *exercise* is more necessary than anything else to the preservation of the health of the hoof. It aids the circulation of blood within the foot, and, therefore, the growth of the horn. Horses which perform hard, regular work have, as a rule, better hoofs than those which stand the greater part of the time in the stable. Poulticing hoofs with clay, bran, linseed-meal, or white-rock, or standing them in water is unnecessary if they have had proper care, but will sometimes be of benefit when the hoofs have been neglected, and especially so for front hoofs. The latter are more exposed to drying influences, and the shoes prevent the moistening process by keeping the hoofs partially or completely removed from contact with the earth. *Oiling alone is not sufficient to soften horn,* but must always be preceded by permeation of the horn with water. **Oiling without first cleansing the hoof is useless, because this soon produces a greasy crust underneath which the horn is crisp and brittle.**

The surest sign of cleanliness of a hoof is the appearance of the natural color of the horn, the latter appearing translucent even after the hoof-ointment has been applied; therefore, blackened hoof-ointments should not be used. When hoofs are exposed to too much moisture (muddy roads, melting snow, etc.) an addition of wax or common yellow rosin to the hoof-ointment is recommended to prevent too great softening of the horn. *No hoof-ointment has any direct influence upon the growth of the horn.*

Inasmuch as it is a fact that the very best shoeing injures the hoof, it is advisable to allow horses to go barefoot whenever it is possible. This applies especially to horses that from any cause are thrown out of service, presupposing, of course, that the nature of the hoofs will allow them to go barefoot.

PART III.

CHAPTER VII.

GENERAL REMARKS CONCERNING THE SHOEING OF DEFECTIVE HOOFS AND LAME HORSES.

THE boundary between health and disease of the hoof is difficult to determine, especially when we have to deal with minor defects of structure or shape of the hoof. Ordinarily, we first consider a hoof diseased when it causes lameness. However, we know that diseases of the hoof may exist without lameness. Therefore, a hoof should be regarded as diseased or defective when the nature of the horn, the form of the hoof, or the parts enclosed by it, deviate from what we consider as normal or healthy (see page 81), whether the service of the animal is influenced by it or not.

Front hoofs become diseased or defective more readily than hind hoofs, because they bear greater weight, have more slanting walls, and are more exposed to drying influences. **All normally wry hoofs and acute-angled hoofs become more readily diseased than regular and upright (stumpy) hoofs.**

The *indications* of the various diseases of the hoof are discussed in the following chapters. We shall in this chapter undertake only a brief general discussion of *inflammation of the pododerm.* This inflammation, known as **pododermatitis,** always manifests itself by *lameness* and, under closer examination of the foot, by *increased warmth, pain,* and *stronger pulsation of the digital* and *plantar arteries.* The pain produces either a *timid, shortened* (sore) *gait,* or well-marked *lameness,* especially upon *hard* ground. Increased sensitiveness of the pododerm is detected by compression of the hoof with the pincers (hoof-testers), or with greater certainty by lightly tapping the hoof. The increased warmth of a part or of the entire hoof is detected by feeling with the hand. Intense pain and greatly increased warmth, with a moderate, diffuse swelling of the soft parts between the hoof and fetlock-joint, indicate suppuration within the hoof.

The examination of horses lame in the feet must always be cautious and searching, and should begin with the moving and judging of the horse as already described on page 90. The faults detected in the hoof or in the shoeing, the pain and increased warmth of the hoof, will not leave us in doubt as to whether the animal is lame in the hoof or not. However, should there be a doubt, we must carefully examine all the joints and tendons of the foot and, if necessary, of the limb above, and observe the animal's manner of travelling at a walk and at a trot, on soft and on hard ground, in a straight line and in a circle.

The **removal of the shoe** should be performed with **greatest caution.** Under certain conditions the second shoe should not be removed until the first has been replaced. The same caution must be observed in paring the hoof, which is to be regarded as a part of the examination of the hoof. The paring of a hoof for this purpose often differs somewhat from the preparation of a sound hoof for the shoe, and while it is necessary because it frequently furnishes the first trustworthy indication of the trouble, it must be done with circumspection and intelligence.

The *causes* of diseases of the hoof are very numerous, for many external influences act injuriously upon the hoof. In addition to too great dryness, want of care (neglected shoeing), and premature, unreasonable, cruel use of the horse, should be mentioned particularly *injudicious dressing of the hoof and direct and indirect faults in the shoeing*. The pododerm, shut in between the hard os pedis and the stiff, unyielding horn capsule, is frequently exposed to bruising and other injuries. from which arise most of the defects of the hoof itself. All these things lead, under certain conditions, to lameness.

Treatment.—First of all, the discovered causes should be removed, or, if this is not possible, as is frequently the case, they should be ameliorated. Very often the lameness may be removed by proper shoeing, a change in the animal's work, and better care of the hoof. When there is intense inflammation within the foot, the shoe should be removed for a few days. When the inflammation is moderate and confined to a small area, it is usually sufficient to alter the shoeing by regulating unnatural relations of height in the different parts of the wall, and by removing all superfluous horn from the wall and sole (to a less degree from the frog), partly for the purpose of rendering the horn capsule more yielding, and partly to make the poultices which are used more effective. The shoe is then to be so applied that the diseased region will be *relieved of the body-weight,* and will remain free from all pressure from the shoe. This can be done partly by making the underlying branch of the shoe somewhat wider and longer than the other, and partly by cutting down the bearing-edge of the wall where this is possible without weakening it too much, otherwise by concaving or beating down the upper surface of the shoe. By reason of the fact that the posterior half of the hoof is the seat of most diseases of the hoof, it is to be recommended that the nail-holes in shoes used in these diseases be placed as far as possible in the anterior half of the shoe, and in some special cases distributed evenly around the toe. Among shoes suitable for diseased hoofs

FIG. 185.

Bar-shoe for right foot.

the bar-shoe (Fig. 185) holds the first place, because it renders superfluous many other shoes specially designed for various diseases of the hoof. It is made like an ordinary flat shoe, except that it requires a somewhat longer piece of iron; the ends of the branches are bent inward over a dull corner of the anvil, bevelled, laid one over the other, and welded together to form the bar. The width and thickness of the bar should be the same as of the rest of the shoe, and its frog-surface should be slightly concave.

The *bar-shoe is valuable, because* it protects from pressure diseased sections of the wall which have been laid free, allows part of the body-weight to be borne by the frog, and restores normal activity to the disturbed physiological movements of the foot. By using it we can either gain a more extensive bearing-surface for the hoof, or can make it easier for the surface that bears the weight to do the work. If on account of *weakness* of the bearing-surface of the hoof, or from any other cause, we wish to distribute the body-weight over the entire plantar surface of the foot with the exception of the painful region, we add a *leather sole* to the bar-shoe.

In this case it is necessary to place holes in the ends of the branches of the shoe, so that we may rivet the leather firmly to the shoe with small nails. The shoe should be made somewhat wider than the hoof, and the clips somewhat higher than usual. After fitting the shoe the grooves for the clips are cut in the leather, the latter is riveted to the shoe, and all leather projecting beyond the outer edge of the shoe is trimmed away. The lacunæ of the frog and other concavities of the sole are then thickly smeared with wood-tar and afterwards filled up with oakum to such a degree that the packing will bear some of the body-weight when the shoe and leather sole are in position. This packing is of great importance, because it prevents the filtering in from behind of sand and slime, preserves the toughness and pliability of the horn, breaks shock, and produces a gradual expansion of the posterior half of the hoof. Before nailing the shoe to the foot the leather sole should be soaked in water.

Classification of Diseases of the Hoof.

INFLAMMATIONS OF THE PODODERM.

1, Nailing (pricking and close nailing); 2, street-nail; 3, calk-wounds; 4, corns (bruised sole); 5, bruised heels; 6, laminitis (founder); 7, keraphyllocele (tumor of horny leaves).

DEFECTS OF THE HORN CAPSULE AND LATERAL CARTILAGES.

(*a*) Changes of form: 1, flat hoof and full hoof (dropped sole); 2, upright hoof (stumpy or stubby hoof); 3, contracted hoof; 4, wry hoof; 5, crooked hoof; 6, ossification of the lateral cartilage (side-bone).

(*b*) Disturbances of continuity of the horn capsule: 1, cracks; 2, clefts; 3, loose wall; 4, hollow wall; 5, thrush.

CHAPTER VIII.

INFLAMMATIONS OF THE PODODERM (PODODERMATITIS).

1. Nailing.

Wounds of the velvety tissue of the sole or of the podophyllous tissue of the wall, caused by nails which have been driven into the hoof for the purpose of fastening the shoe, are usually termed " nailing."

We distinguish *direct* and *indirect* nailing; the former is noticed *immediately,* the latter *later.*

In **direct** nailing the nail passes directly into the pododerm (velvety tissue of the sole, podophyllous tissue) ; the wound produced may vary from a simple puncture of the pododerm to chipping of the border of the os pedis, and is **always accompanied by bleeding,** even though it may not always be noticed.

In **indirect** nailing the nail does not pass entirely through the horn capsule, but very close to the sensitive tissues, and crowds the soft horn inward against them. This inward bulging presses upon the pododerm and causes inflammation and lameness, which may not manifest themselves for several days.

Symptoms.—The first symptom of direct nailing is **instant pain** indicated by flinching or a jerking of the limb, showing that the nail has taken a wrong course, and then a more or less profuse hemorrhage. Usually the blood flows from the nail-hole, or the nail when withdrawn may merely show a blood-stain at its point; however, internal bleeding may occur without any external manifestations. The symptoms of indirect nailing are entirely different. In this case *pain does not arise immediately,* but later, sometimes as soon as the horse attempts to bear his weight upon the shod foot. In the latter case, on holding up the opposite foot the animal sways backward and throws his weight upon the holder, or becomes restless. As a

166

rule, the consequences of indirect nailing are first manifested after two or three days, infrequently from the eighth to the fourteenth day, as inflammation within the hoof and lameness, at which time a careful examination will usually reveal increased warmth of the hoof, pain upon pressure with the hoof-testers and on tapping the hoof lightly, some swelling of the entire foot, increased pulsation of the digital arteries, and unwillingness of the animal to place all or perhaps any of its weight upon the foot.

Suspicion of nailing should be entertained if the shoeing be recent, the hoof appear too small in relation to the body-weight, the walls have been thinned by rasping or have been broken away, or if the nails have been driven too high or very irregularly.

Causes.—The most common causes are mistakes in shoeing. In the majority of cases the cause is a disregard of the rule that the **nails should penetrate the white line** (see pages 118, 119 and 130, heavy type). 1, Using badly-punched shoes; 2, excessive paring and shortening of the hoof; 3, weakening of the lower border of the wall by excessive rasping away of the outside (Fig. 187, *c*); 4, mistakes in fitting the shoe, especially applying shoes that are too narrow, letting the toe-clips too deep into the horn, by which the nail-holes near the toe, instead of falling upon the white line, are carried back upon the edge of the sole, or using shoes in which the nail-holes are too wide or improperly directed; 5, using nails that are split, incomplete, badly formed and bevelled, and too large; 6, starting nails too deep or with the bevel on the outside, or drawing them too tight. As occasional causes may be mentioned: 7, old nail-stubs in the horn; 8, walls that are very thin or broken away; 9, a soft, crumbling wall, which alters the sound and feeling of the nail as it is driven, and makes it difficult to judge of its course; 10, restlessness of the animal while being shod.

Examination.—Press with the hoof-testers upon the sole and clinches; tap lightly upon the clinches. If these acts cause pain, there can be little doubt that the nail is responsible for the damage. Remove the shoe by drawing each nail separately and carefully.. Examine the nails with reference to their direction and size, as well as to staining with blood, blood-serum, or pus. Immediately after removing the shoe, look for the point of entrance of each nail into the hoof, and if a nail-hole be found upon the edge of the sole (Fig. 187, *b*) instead of in the white line, it is highly probable that the nail which passed

Fig. 187.

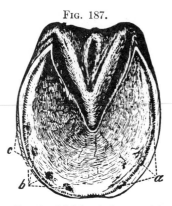

Fig. 186.

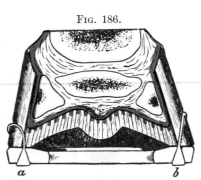

Cross-section of a shod hoof, the hoof-skin or pododerm being in red: *a*, indirect nailing where backsetting has been overdone and has bent the nail; *b*, nail properly placed and of correct shape.

Front hoof deficient in horn: *a*, right position of the nail-holes in the white line; *b*, faulty position inside of the white line; *c*, wall weakened by excessive rasping.

in at that place pressed upon the sensitive tissues of the foot. Every nail-hole should then be searched by passing a clean new nail into it and pressing its point towards the soft tissues at various depths; any indication of pain caused by this act is pretty sure proof of nailing. It stands to reason that the character of the nail-holes in the shoe should be closely examined.

Treatment.—When the foot has sustained an ordinary simple prick with a nail, the latter should be left out and the hole well filled with wax. As a rule, no serious results follow.

In severe direct nailing the entire shoeing should be most carefully examined, and only after everything is found to be right, and the shoe fits in such a manner that the nails can only penetrate the wall from the white line, can it be regarded as correct. The offending nail-hole is then to be closed with wax. According to the intensity of the wound we may expect a more or less pronounced inflammation of the pododerm, and this is to be combated by resting the animal and cooling the foot.

If the wound is clean and recent, enlarging the opening in the horn by cutting and boring can have no reasonable object; the wound by such an act will not be made smaller, but larger.

Frequently, however, the wound is not observed or suspected until the pain has become very intense (indirect nailing, nail-pressure); in such cases the offending nail when withdrawn is apt to be covered with pus or a dark, thin, ill-smelling liquid. In such a case the liquid, whatever its nature may be, must be given free escape. In order to accomplish this it is entirely sufficient to cut away a section of the wall from the nail-hole outward, not greater than the width of the little finger, and then to assist in the discharge of the pus by placing the foot in a warm bath; it is entirely wrong, in fact, reprehensible, to remove all horn of the wall and sole which has been loosened from the soft parts by the suppurative process. After the escape of the inflammatory fluids, the wall and sole will form the best-fitting and most suitable protective dressing for the diseased region until it has secreted new horn. If, after removal of the nail and pus, the pain does not diminish, warm disinfecting baths of one to two parts of creolin, or the same amount of lysol, to one hundred parts of water at a temperature of about 90° F. will be of especial benefit; they will not only soften the horn, but by their moisture and warmth will directly diminish the pain and have a healing influence upon the suppurating surfaces. The warm baths must actually *be warm and be kept warm.* Antiseptic solutions at room temperature are much less efficient.

If the pain has not been very pronounced, or if it has been greatly alleviated by two or three warm baths, then, as a rule, it is sufficient to put a few drops of creolin upon the inflamed surface, and to close the opening with oakum (carbolized oakum or carbolized cotton is better).

The horse which has been nailed will be again perfectly serviceable after a few days if shod with a shoe which does **not press** upon the inflamed region. *The shoe does not press when it rests only upon the bearing-edge of the wall, when the white line and the edge of the sole are entirely free of the shoe, and no nails are driven in the immediate vicinity of the wound.*

Even though, as we have seen, nailing in the great majority of cases is not particularly serious to the horse and owner, yet we should never forget that tetanus (lockjaw), a disease which is nearly always fatal to horses, may follow. Nailing, however insignificant it may seem, may under conditions lead to the death of the horse.

2. Street-Nail.

The *condition* caused by accidental injury of the sensitive structures covered by the horny sole, such as the velvety tissue of the sole and frog, plantar cushion, perforans tendon, navicular bone, os pedis, or the pedal articulation, by sharp objects, especially nails, is called "penetrating street-nail," or simply "street-nail." The resistance of the ground to the weight of the body drives these penetrating objects through the sole or frog into the foot.

Hind hoofs are more often affected than fore-hoofs. A favorite point of entrance is the lateral lacuna of the frog. Street-nail is favored by excessive thinning of the sole and frog.

Symptoms.—The symptoms are, as a rule, sudden pain followed by lameness. The first assistance is usually sought in the shoeing-shop. If the cause of lameness be found to be a penetrating nail, piece of glass, or other pointed foreign body, it must be *carefully drawn out*, in doing which we should remove the *entire object*, not allowing pieces to break off and remain in the wound. Since it is always important to know in what direction and how deep the foreign body has penetrated, in order to be able to estimate the gravity of the wound, it is advisable in all cases to preserve the penetrating body, that it may be shown to the veterinarian, in case his services are required.

Fig. 188.

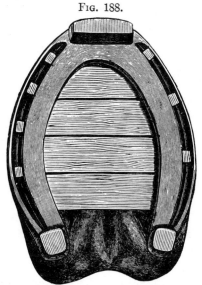

Shod hind foot, with splint dressing.

In slight injuries to the velvety tissue of the sole or frog, accompanied with moderate pain, it is of no benefit to enlarge the opening, though the horn of the sole or frog should be thinned for the space of an inch or more around the wound, followed by cooling applications. Deep, penetrating wounds accompanied with intense pain require the attention of a veterinarian.

Often some form of dressing is necessary, and this is usually held in place by a special shoe. For slight injuries, such *splint-dressings* as are shown in Figs. 188 and 189 are sufficient. Whether such a dressing be applied to the front or hind feet, the shoe should be *well concaved* upon the hoof-surface. The dressing is held in place by thin splints of tough wood, which are firmly wedged between the shoe and hoof.

FIG. 189.

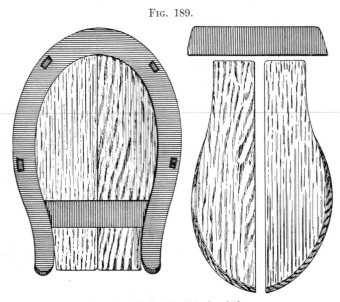

A practical "splint shoe" for hospital use.

In those rare cases in which it is necessary to maintain continuous pressure upon the seat of the wound, and to protect the entire plantar surface of the hoof, a *covered shoe* (Figs. 190 and 191) is recommended. This shoe is provided with a sheet-iron cover, having at the toe a spur which fits into a corresponding hole in the toe of the shoe, and fastened at the heels by means of screw heel-calks.

3. Calk Wounds of the Coronet.

All tread-wounds of the coronet, caused by the calks of the opposite shoe, by the shoes of other horses, or by forging, are known as calk wounds, or simply as "calking." The injury itself is either a bruise or a bruised wound, followed by inflammation of the coronary cushion and an interruption in the formation of horn at that point. It occurs most often in winter

FIG. 190.

FIG. 191.

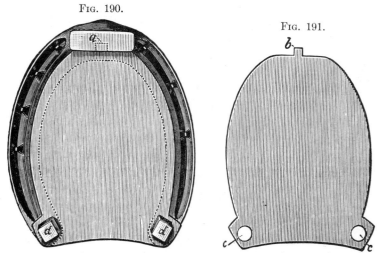

Shoe with cover-plate for street-nail treatment; suitable where pressure-dressing is desired: *a*, hole in the bottom of the toe-calk for reception of spur, *b*, of cover-plate; *c*, holes for reception of screw-calks, *d*, which fasten the cover-plate to the shoe.

from sharp calks, especially on the hind feet. The common seat of the injury is the coronet of the toe and inner side of the foot.

The inflammation terminates either in resolution—that is, passes gradually away, leaving the tissues apparently normal—or in suppuration. The perioplic horn-band, which is usually loosened from the perioplic band by the injury, does not again unite. For this reason, and because of the interruption in the

formation of horn at the seat of injury, there results a transverse depression or cleft in the wall.

The shoeing has to deal only with the lameness that may
be present as a result of the calking. The section of the wall
containing the lesion should be shortened, so that it will not
press upon the shoe. Serious calk wounds, as a rule, require
treatment by a veterinarian.

4. Corns (Bruised Sole).

The expression " corns " is applied to nearly all bruises of
the pododerm of the posterior half of the foot, with the exception of the frog, which are apparent to the eye as yellowish,
reddish, or bluish-red discolorations of the horn of the sole and
white line.

The surface of the pododerm (fleshy leaves and villi) is
chiefly involved, and almost without exception there is rupture
of small blood-vessels and an outpouring of blood between the
pododerm and the horn. The blood penetrates the horn-tubes
and causes the above-mentioned staining. By subsequent growth
of horn these stained patches are carried downward, and are
finally uncovered and brought to sight in paring the hoof.

The seat of corns is either on the fleshy leaves of the
quarters, or on the velvety tissue of the sole in the angle between
the wall and the bar, or on the fleshy leaves of the bars. Thus
we distinguish *corns of the wall, sole, and bars.*

Corns affect chiefly the front hoofs, and more often the
inner half than the outer. Unshod feet are seldom affected.

According to the intensity of the lesions we distinguish:

1. *Dry Corns.*—The red-stained horn is dry, and there is
seldom lameness.

2. *Suppurating Corns.*—They are the result of intense
bruising followed by inflammation. The pus is either thin and
dark grayish in color, denoting a superficial inflammation of
the pododerm, or yellowish and thick, denoting a deep in-

flammation of the pododerm. In the latter case a veterinarian should be called. Lameness is usually pronounced.

3. *Chronic Corns.*—In this case there is vivid discoloration of horn in all possible hues. The horn is either soft, moist, and lardy, or crumbling, cracked, and at times bloody. The inner surface of the horn capsule has lost its normal character, and is covered with horny swellings or nodules (Fig. 192, *a*). Sometimes the wing of the os pedis on that side has become morbidly enlarged and loosened. A short, cautious gait alternates with well-marked lameness; the latter appears whenever the shoe presses too firmly on the corn, or when the hoof becomes too dry.

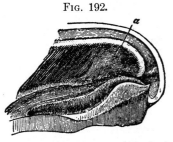

Fig. 192.

The causes, aside from the form and quality of the hoofs and the position of the limbs, lie in injudicious dressing of the hoof and in faulty shoes. Too much trimming of wide and flat hoofs, excessive weakening of the quarters, sole, bars, and frog of all other hoofs, while the

Inner aspect of a quarter of a hoof, showing changes in the horn-leaves due to chronic corns: *a*, horny tumor resulting from the disease.

toe is usually left too long, are the usual causes. Shortening one quarter too much in relation to the other, so that the foot is unbalanced and the lower side overloaded, is a frequent cause. Hollowing the sole and bars excessively and unnecessary thinning of the branches of the sole in the search for corns are also causes.

Among faulty shoes we may mention those not level on the hoof-surface, trough-shaped, too short in the branches, shoes which do not completely cover the bearing-surface of the hoof, or whose bearing-surface at the ends of the branches is directed downward and inward so that the quarters are squeezed together when the weight is put on the foot. Insufficient concaving of the shoe is often an exciting cause of corns in flat feet and in those with dropped soles. A well-formed shoe which does not rest firmly upon the hoof, or which has been shifted as a result of careless nailing, may as readily cause bruising of the quarters as neglected shoeing. The latter causes, as a rule, corns of the sole. It is very rarely that corns are caused by stones fastened between the frog and branches of the shoe or in unshod hoofs by pebbles becoming wedged in the white line.

Dryness is particularly injurious to the hoofs, and is in the highest degree favorable to the production of corns. It renders the hoof stiff and inelastic, and first manifests itself by a short, cautious (sore) gait when the horse is first put to work.

Treatment.—First, removal of the causes, by restoring the proper form to the hoof through shortening a toe which is too long (especially apt to be the case in acute-angled hoofs), cutting down quarters which are too high, and carefully removing all dead horn from the branches of the sole, especially in acute-angled hoofs.

Deeply digging out a small area of blood-stained horn is injurious. It is much better to thin the horn of the entire branch of the sole uniformly, in doing which we should avoid wounding the velvety tissue of the sole or drawing blood.

The proper shoe is the **bar-shoe,** except when both cartilages are ossified. The pressure should not be taken from the quarters unless they are sore.

When there is a *suppurating corn,* the shoe should be left off several days. A *chronic corn* should be protected continuously from pressure by the shoe. This is accomplished by using a bar-shoe with leather sole. *A three-quarter shoe is not sufficient to properly protect a hoof affected with a chronic corn, if the animal must perform exacting labor on hard roads.*

The care of the hoof consists in keeping it cool, moderately moist, and pliant.

5. Inflammation of the Heels.

Inflammation of the bulbs of the plantar cushion (heels) is usually caused by such external influences as bruising. It occurs in both shod and unshod feet. The symptoms are: increased warmth, pain and swelling, sometimes infiltration of the tissues with blood, accompanied by a short, cautious gait, or, if only one foot is affected, by well-marked lameness.

The *most frequent causes* are: going barefoot upon hard (frozen), uneven ground; shoeing hoofs having low heels with flat shoes that are too short; sometimes too much frog-pressure by the bar of a bar-shoe; forging and grabbing.

The treatment first indicated is a cooling application in the form of an ice-poultice, or a soaking in cold water. Later, astringent (drying) applications are of benefit, especially if the perioplic horn-ring has partially loosened from the bulbs of the heels; for example, a weak solution in water of sulphate of copper (1 to 20), followed by the application of a shoe with heel-calks, which is quite long in the branches and *which must not press upon the wall of the quarters.*

6. Laminitis (Founder).

By this name we designate a peculiar inflammation of the pododerm at the toe. It arises suddenly in well-nourished and apparently healthy horses, following excessive work or long-continued rest in the stable, and frequently leads to a decided change of form of the hoof.

The disease is always accompanied with intense pain. It most often affects both front feet, more rarely all four feet, or only one foot. In the first case the two front feet are planted far in advance of the body, and the hind feet well forward under the belly. When all four feet are affected, travelling is exceedingly difficult, often impossible; in this case there is nearly always a high fever over the entire body.

The seat of the disease is in the fleshy leaves about the toe, more rarely upon the side walls and quarters. Depending upon the intensity of the inflammation, the fleshy leaves are more or less loosened from the horny leaves, as a result of which there is a change of position of the os pedis, with a simultaneous

sinking of the coronet at the toe.   This produces a change of
form of the hoof.   The quarters become higher.   Rings form
upon the wall, and their course is quite characteristic of the
disease.   At the toe these rings are quite close to one another,
but as they pass back towards the quarters they gradually
separate from one another and recede from the coronary band
(Figs. 193, 194, and 195).

The wall at the toe is sunken just under the coronet; its
lower part, on the contrary, is thrust forward.   *Later, the white*

Fig. 193.

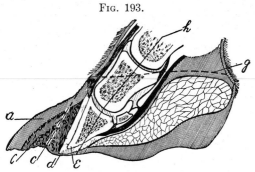

Vertical longitudinal section of a foot altered by chronic laminitis: *a*, hollow wall at toe
thrust forward; *b*, leafy layer much thickened and crumbling ("seedy-toe"); *c*, dotted line
showing limit to which the toe may be rasped away in shoeing; *d*, dropped sole; *e*, atrophy
of lower sharp edge of os pedis; *g*, dotted line indicating the height of the perioplic band; *h*,
foot axis.

line becomes pathologically widened.   The horn of the white
line is dry, crumbling, and easily broken down, so that a break
in continuity (crack) is apt to occur between the wall and sole,
and lead to the formation of a *hollow wall* (" seedy toe ").
Where the inflammation is moderate and is not repeated, healing
usually takes place and the horn grows down regularly and in
normal direction from the coronet.   However, a rather brittle
condition of the horn remains permanently.   If, on the contrary, the inflammation was very severe or repeated several
times, the horny sole becomes flat just in front of the point of
the frog as a result of the sinking of the os pedis, or it may even

drop below the level of the wall (full hoof, dropped sole). Indeed, it even happens at times that the toe of the os pedis perforates the horny sole just in front of the point of the frog.

Fig. 194.   Fig. 195.

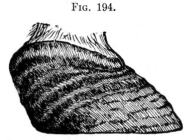 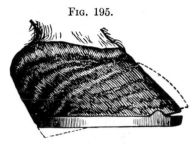

Foundered foot (chronic laminitis), before dressing.

Foundered foot, dressed and shod. The dotted lines indicate its form before being dressed,—*i.e.*, as shown in Fig. 194.

The wall at the toe, which was previously but little altered in form, is now thrust prominently forward.

The inflammation of the pododerm may under certain conditions and by skilful veterinary treatment be removed, so that the characteristic changes of form and quality of the hoof will not occur. But if this is not accomplished, as is often the case, the disease will be obstinate, and permanent m o r b i d changes of the horn capsule take place.

A horse in such a condition can be used, but the

Fig. 196.

A hoof altered by chronic laminitis; shod with an open flat shoe: *a*, wall at the toe does not bear on the shoe; *b*, clip at the end of the branch to oppose the tendency of the shoe to slip forward when half worn out.

gait will be short and stiff. The hoofs are shuffled forward and set heels first to the ground, a manner of travelling that rapidly wears away the branches of the shoe.

In dressing a foundered hoof the outer circumference of

the sole is the guide. The thick projecting wall at the toe may
be removed with the rasp without injuring the foot. The sole
should be spared, but the quarters should be lowered to improve
the setting of the foot to the ground.

The choice of the shoe will depend upon the shape and
nature of the sole. If this is still concave, an ordinary shoe
may be used. If, however, the sole is flat or dropped, it must
be protected by an open shoe with a broad web, or with a

FIG. 197.

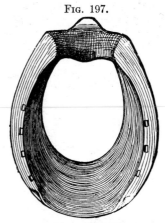

A well-covered (wide-webbed) bar-shoe,
with two lateral toe-clips and an end-clip,
for a foundered foot.

FIG. 198.

An open shoe for a foundered foot with a
dropped sole.

bar-shoe (Fig. 197), which is of especial value when the bearing-edge of the wall is weak or broken away.

As long as there is pain on pressure about the toe there
should be no toe-clip, but two side-clips. The wall between
these clips should be lowered a tenth to an eighth of an inch
to prevent pressure of the shoe upon the sensitive tissues of
the toe (Fig. 195). The nails should be as small as possible
and placed well back towards the quarters. No nail should be
driven in the wall at the toe when there is separation of sole
and wall at the toe (hollow wall, seedy-toe).

The shoes of horses affected with founder often work

forward as a result of the animals travelling upon their heels. To prevent this evil, clips may be raised at the ends of the branches of an open shoe, or one clip in the middle of the bar, in case a bar-shoe is used (Fig. 197).

7. Keraphyllocele (Horn Tumor).

A keraphyllocele is a more or less sharply bounded horn tumor projecting from the inner surface of the wall.

Its occurrence is rare. Its favorite seat is at the toe. It rarely causes lameness. It can only be diagnosed with certainty when it extends downward to the lower border of the wall. In this case there may be seen a half-moon-shaped thickening of the white line which rounds inward upon the edge of the sole, and is of a waxen color. Frequently the horn at this place crumbles away, leaving a more or less dark-colored cavity from which there sometimes escapes a small quantity of dark-grayish pus.

Causes.—Chronic inflammation of the podophyllous tissue, resulting from compression or bruising. Keraphyllocele frequently follows a complete toe-crack of long duration, or a deep calk-wound at the coronet.

Prognosis.—Unfavorable, whether there is lameness or not. If there is no lameness it is very apt to arise later, and if lameness is already present it can only be removed by an operation, which should be performed by a veterinarian. A return of the lameness following hard work at a trot upon hard roads is always to be feared.

Fig. 199.

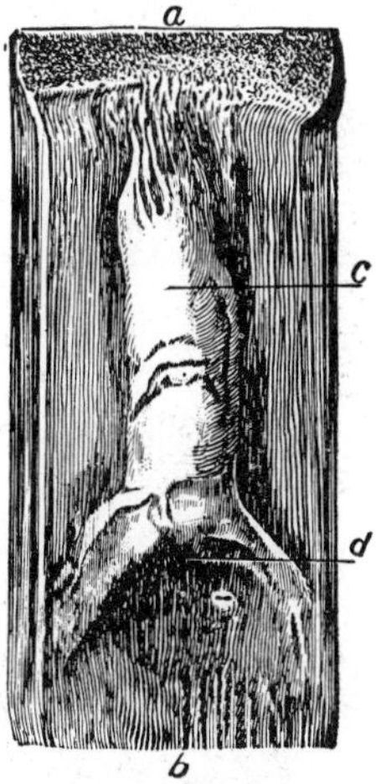

A section of wall at the toe showing a Keraphyllocele (horn-leaf tumor): *a*, coronary border; *b*, plantar border; *c*, body of tumor *d*, base of tumor presenting funnel-shaped opening discharging pus.

Shoeing.—An ordinary shoe well concaved underneath the inflamed region, which should be relieved of all pressure.*

---

* Should lameness persist, it will be necessary to remove a strip of the wall from the plantar border to the coronet in order to remove the horn tumor. The fleshy leaves which have secreted the tumor must be extirpated and the surface of the os pedis well scraped, or the growth will return.

CHAPTER IX.

DEFECTS OF THE HOOF.

A. Changes of Form.

1. THE FLAT AND THE FULL HOOF (DROPPED SOLE).

(*a*) *Flat Hoof.*—A flat hoof is one whose toe and side walls are *inclined very obliquely* to the ground surface, and whose sole is *on a level* with the bearing-surface of the wall.

It exists most often in horses bred in low-lying, marshy countries.

Frequently the frog is well developed, and projects considerably beyond the level of the wall. The branches of the sole sink perceptibly under the weight of the body, much more than in better-formed hoofs.

Preparing the Hoof for the Shoe.—The rule is to **spare** the plantar surface of the foot. After removing from the sole what little loose horn there may be, level the usually deficient bearing-surface of the wall with the rasp. The outer border of the wall, especially at the toe, should be rounded off rather more strongly than usual, because the toe requires and will bear considerable shortening. Outward bendings of the lower border of the wall should be removed as far as it is practicable to do so.

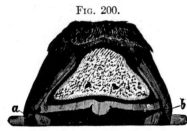

FIG. 200.

Cross-section of a shod flat foot: *a*, sufficiently high bearing-edge of wall, and a horizontal bearing-surface on the shoe; *b*, insufficient height of bearing-edge of wall, and therefore a corresponding downward and inward inclination of the bearing-surface of the shoe.

The shoe, which should be rather wider in the web and thicker than usual, should have its bearing-surface shaped to

182

correspond to the bearing-surface of the wall; that is, if the bearing-surface of the wall is below the margin of the sole (the sole of the foot being uppermost), then the bearing-surface of the shoe should incline downward and inward (Fig. 200, *b*). The bearing-surface of the branches, however, must always remain horizontal. The shoe always requires deep concaving, especially along the inner branch of the sole. If the quarters are weak, the walls defective, or there are corns, cracks, loose walls, or other diseases of the hoof, a **bar-shoe** should be selected.

(*b*) *Full Hoof* (Dropped Sole).—A full hoof is one whose sole instead of being concave is convex,—that is, bulges beyond the bearing-surface of the wall. It either arises gradually from a flat hoof or is the result of laminitis (founder). In full hoofs the lower surface of the os pedis is of the same shape as the horny sole.

The preparation of a full hoof for the shoe consists merely in removing all loose horn. In case the dropping of the sole is very pronounced, the bearing surface of the wall should be built up artificially with Defay's hoof cement. The shoe should be light, but broad in the web, and furnished with a more or less deep concaving, which extends from the inner edge of the web to the outer edge of the shoe, and corresponds in shape to the bulging of the sole. By reason of the deficiency of the wall, the **bar-shoe** deserves the preference over an open shoe. It is frequently necessary to apply toe- and heel-calks to remove the hoof from contact with the ground. The nails should be thinner and longer than usual, and a more secure position of the shoe may be secured without injury to the hoof by drawing up two side-clips.

Flat and full hoofs are **incurable.** Shoeing is of benefit only in rendering such horses serviceable. Soles that are soft and sensitive should be smeared with crude turpentine or pine-tar, though unusual sensitiveness calls for a leather sole. Horses with full hoofs should not be driven faster than a walk over hard roads. During long-continued spells of wet weather softening of these hoofs should be prevented by smearing the soles with a hoof-ointment containing resin.

2. THE UPRIGHT OR STUMPY HOOF.

The upright or stumpy hoof is that form in which the quarters, with relation to the toe, are too long (too high). The wall at the toe stands very steep, in some cases perpendicular, and is strongly worn away by standing and travelling.

FIG. 201.

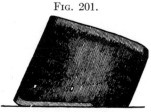

Upright or stumpy hoof, shod with a "tip."

Causes.—1. The upright hoof is peculiar to the " standing under " position (Fig. 53, page 66) and to the so-called bear-foot (Fig. 70, page 72).

2. It arises also as a result of all those alterations in the direction of the limbs which tend to remove the quarters from contact with the ground (contraction of the flexor tendons, spavin,—Fig. 202).

3. It may arise gradually from neglect of the hoofs of horses running barefoot.

4. It may arise from excessive shortening of the toe in relation to the quarters.

Shoeing.—The forms of hoofs mentioned in class 1 should be left as they are. The hoofs that fall under class 2 should be dressed and shod until a more natural setting down of the foot is secured. This is brought about by sparing the quarters, and applying a shoe with thickened branches or with heel-calks. Where the service of the animal is

FIG. 202.

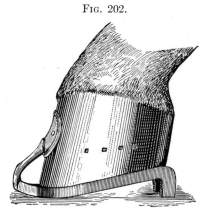

Beaked shoe for stilt-foot.

exacting and upon hard streets, the toes, especially of the hind shoes, may be made more durable by welding in steel plates. Besides, the shoe should be moderately *base-wide* around the toe,—that is, should be bevelled downward and outward, should have a *strong toe-clip,* and should be *quite concave at the toe* and *rolled.* (Figs. 203 and 204). Should the hoof tip forward whenever the weight is thrown upon the limb, a shoe with a

FIG. 203.   FIG. 204.

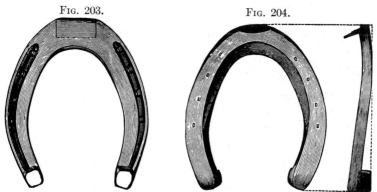

Shoe for stumpy hoofs, viewed from ground-surface, hoof-surface, and in profile.

spur projecting from the centre of the toe, and turning back and pressing upon the wall just underneath the coronary band, will be of service (Fig. 202).

Only those upright hoofs which are the result of the causes mentioned in 3 and 4 are to be dressed as ordinary hoofs, and if the service required is not too exacting they should be shod with tips (Fig. 201), or with shoes with thinned branches.

3. THE CONTRACTED HOOF.

A hoof which has deviated from its normal form in such a manner that its posterior half, either in part or as a whole, is too narrow, is a contracted hoof. The walls of the quarters assume an abnormally oblique direction downward and inward towards the median line of the hoof.

When contraction affects only one quarter, it is called *uni-lateral contraction,* or abnormal wryness (Fig. 211).

The buttresses are usually very much prolonged and press upon the frog and cause it to shrink. The bars no longer run in the natural straight direction from the point of the frog backward and outward, but describe a circle passing outward, backward, and inward.

Contraction affects front feet, especially those of the *acute-angled* form, more often than hind feet. In order to determine whether or not a hoof is too narrow, we should always examine the frog and its lateral lacunæ. If the frog is small and narrow, and the lateral lacunæ very narrow and deep, there can be no doubt but that the hoof is too narrow (contracted).

FIG. 205.

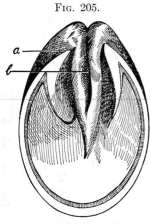

A fore-hoof with bilateral contraction of the quarters: *a,* spur of horn prolonged from the buttress, which compresses the frog; *b,* narrow median lacuna of the frog.

The causes, aside from too little exercise, are chiefly errors in shoeing, such as weakening the posterior half of the hoof, leaving too long a toe, either neglecting to remove the spurs of horn which grow from the buttresses and press upon the frog, or removing them incompletely, and using shoes whose branches are either *too wide apart* or are inclined downward and inward, so that under the weight of the body *the heels are squeezed together* and contraction is favored.

Prevention and Treatment.—First, it should be borne in mind *that whatever exercises moderate pressure upon the sole, frog, and bars tends to expand the hoof.* The action and value of the various shoes, frog-, and sole-pads, are measured by this rule. For this reason a shoe with heel-calks is never advisable if an open flat shoe without other means of relief can be used.

Furthermore, since contraction is the parent of nearly all diseases of the hoof (corns, quarter-cracks, bar-cracks, thrush of the frog), we should use the greatest care to **prevent** it by dressing the hoof as described on pages 98 to 103, using flat shoes **with a horizontal bearing-surface for the quarters,** giving **abundant exercise, preventing drying out of the horn,** and allowing the animal to go barefoot whenever possible. *Where the contraction is but slight* the foregoing rules will be found sufficient.

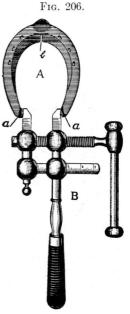

FIG. 206.

In very pronounced contraction, where the hoof is not acute-angled, an expansive shoe with clips raised at the ends of the branches to press against the buttresses may prove very advantageous; but under no conditions should violence be used in expanding the heels with the expanding-screw. This is an act of extreme delicacy, and should be performed only by experienced veterinarians.

In very pronounced contraction of one or both quarters of hoofs of every degree of obliquity we may obtain a continuous expansive action by the use of one of the numerous V-shaped springs, of which the *Chadwick spring* is the best (Fig. 207 and 208). After levelling the wall and thinning the branches of the sole, the points of the spring are set against the **buttresses,** the apex of the

A, Defay's shoe for expanding the quarters of a hoof: *a*, clip apposed to the buttress; *b*, slot sawed at the toe to weaken the shoe; *B*, screw for expanding the Defay's shoe.

spring moved to and fro till the points have bored well into the horn, when the apex is laid against the sole at the toe, the sole filled with tar and oakum and covered by a leather sole, and a bar-shoe applied. If the contraction be less pronounced, or if the frog be much shrunken we may place a Chadwick spring beneath a rubber bar-pad with a short shoe. The spring may be stiffened from shoeing to shoeing, first by introducing the ferrule at the apex of the spring and later by shifting the ferrule toward the shoulder (Figs. 207, *b,* and 208, *b*).

For contracted hoofs of the *acute-angled form* we use the bar-shoe, and if there are other diseases of the hoof present, or if we wish a more rapid and continuous expansive action, we use also a leather sole with foot-packing with or without a

FIG. 208.

FIG. 207.

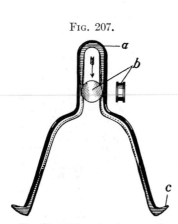

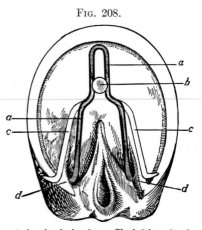

The Chadwick spring for expanding contracted quarters: *a*, apex of spring; *b*, ferrule to stiffen the spring; *c*, point which is buried in a buttress of the hoof.

A fore-hoof showing a Chadwick spring in proper position: *a*, Chadwick spring; *b*, ferrule to stiffen spring as desired; *c*, uncompressed spring before it has been engaged against the buttresses; *d*, buttresses in which points of spring are buried.

buttress spring. A foul frog should be properly cleansed, and then disinfected with pine-tar thinned with alcohol or crude wood-vinegar (pyroligneous acid).

Further curative measures are: turning the horse out without shoes (expensive and seldom practicable); applying tips; using shoes the bearing-surface of whose branches inclines downward and outward (unilateral contraction requires but one branch to be so constructed); hoof-pads of rubber (Figs. 145,

146, and 147), straw, rope, cork, hoof-cement, etc. Special forms of contraction are distinguished, and are as follows:

(*a*) *The Contraction of Wide Hoofs.*—This contraction is manifest as a concavity or groove in the wall just below the coronet, usually at the quarters, though sometimes extending entirely around the foot parallel to the coronary band (Fig. 209). Pain is produced in the contracted area by lightly tapping the horn, but not by moderate pressure with the hoof-testers.

Green horses with wide hoofs, just from the pasture, are particularly liable to this form of contraction. As a rule, the lameness does not disappear completely until the wall has assumed its natural, straight direction by growing down properly from the coronary band.

In dressing the hoof and apply-ing the *bar-shoe,* care must be taken that the lower border of the wall underneath the painful area is lowered so much that it will not receive direct pressure from the shoe.

(*b*) *Contraction of the Sole.*—This is accompanied by an unnatural direction of the wall. Instead of the wall being straight from the coronet

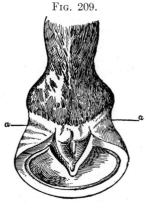

FIG. 209.

Wide fore-hoof with "coronary contraction": (*a*) broad shallow groove in each quarter, and dis-appearing toward the toe.

to the shoe, it describes a curve whose convexity is outward (keg-shaped, claw-shaped when seen from the side) (Fig. 210). The hoof seems constricted (tied in) at the coronet and at its plantar border, the sole is abnormally concave (arched), and the plantar surface of the hoof is considerably shortened from toe to heel. It happens in both shod and unshod horses, with otherwise strong hoofs, but is quite rare. It is occasionally associated with navicular bursitis ("navicular disease").

Causes.—Principally dryness, too little exercise, and shoes without horizontal bearing-surface.

The treatment is correspondingly simple: The shoes should be flat, fitted full all around to coax the wall out at every point, and the outer border bevelled base-wide, so as to furnish a base of support that is wider and longer than the hoof. In moderate contraction of the sole, the bearing-surface of the shoe should be perfectly horizontal, but if the contraction be very pronounced, the entire bearing-surface should incline downward and outward (even at the toe). No toe- or side-clip should be used. The shoe should be reset every two weeks; the sole kept so thin by paring that it will spring under thumb pressure, and kept moist by washing, tubbing or " stopping," and the animal given moderate exercise daily.

FIG. 210.

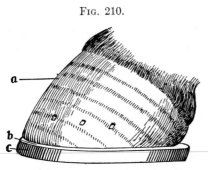

A fore-hoof with a contracted sole, properly shod: *a*, toe convex in profile; *b*, shoe fitted full all around, and "bearing-surface" inclining outward; *c*, outer border bevelled base-wide.

In all forms of contraction of the hoof abundant exercise and the maintenance of the natural pliancy of the horn by daily moistening (washing) with water are absolutely necessary for successful treatment.

4. THE WRY HOOF.

If one side wall and quarter is steep, and the other very slanting or oblique, we term such a hoof a " wry hoof." Such a hoof divided in the middle line presents two very *dissimilar* halves. There are three classes of wry hoofs: 1, normal wry hoofs (see Figs. 63–66); 2, pathological wry hoofs, or hoofs contracted in one quarter (see contracted hoofs); 3, wry hoofs which are the result of improper shortening of the wall and of neglect in horses running barefoot.

Only the second and third classes of wry hoofs require especial attention. First, the more oblique wall must be cut down, and the steep wall spared,—a procedure which differs essentially from that employed in treating the first class, but is, nevertheless, entirely warranted, because these second and third kinds of wry hoofs do not correspond to the direction of the limb.

In order to take weight from the steep wall, we use with advantage a *bar-shoe,* which should be longer and wider than the hoof on its contracted side. In other words, enlarge the base of support by making the branch of the shoe broader. If an entire side wall and quarter is contracted the branch of the shoe beneath must be broad, the border bevelled base-wide, and the branch punched so deeply that the nail-holes will fall upon the white line. In old work-horses any sort of shoe may be used, though a flat shoe serves the purpose best. If a hoof is wry from faulty paring, and

FIG. 211.

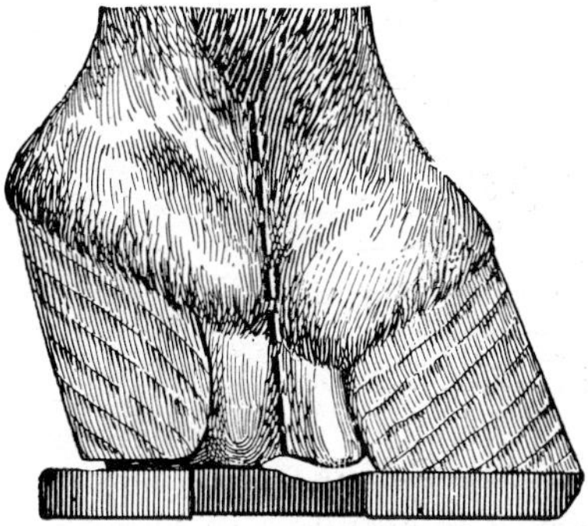

A wry right front foot of the base-wide class, viewed from behind. The bar shoe is fitted full along the contracted inner quarter, and snug on the outside. The inner branch of the frog rests upon the bar of the shoe; the outer branch is free. The inner quarter from the last nail back to the frog is free of the shoe.

we cannot at once completely restore the proper relative slant of the two walls by paring alone, we may use a shoe with a thicker branch for the half of the hoof which is too low (too steep).

In colts such wry hoofs can often be cured only by shoeing. The shoe employed for this purpose is so made that the branch underneath the steep(contracted)wall is quite thick, but gradually thins away around the toe to the end of the other branch. In strongly marked cases the thin branch may end at the middle

of the side wall (a three-quarter shoe). This method of shoeing shifts the body-weight upon the slanting wall and restores
the foot to its proper shape in from two to four shoeings.

Causes.—Unequal distribution of the weight in the inner
and outer halves of the foot, in conjunction with excessive
cutting down or wear of the steeper wall. All faults in shoeing
which tend to produce contraction of the heels aid in the formation of a wry foot, especially when these faults directly affect
the steep wall. Neglect of the colt's hoofs during the first
years of life frequently lays the basis for wry foot in later
years. All wry feet are more susceptible to disease than others.

The amount or degree of wryness varies considerably. In a
moderately developed case the steep wall (usually the inner)
will be drawn in at the plantar border of the quarter, presenting
a convex surface between this border and the coronet, and the
adjacent branch of the frog will be more or less shrunken. In
extreme cases the slanting wall (usually the outer) will also be
involved and bent in the opposite direction,—*i.e.,* will be concave (dished) between coronet and lower border (crooked hoof).

Prognosis.—When the degree of wryness corresponds to the
slant of the foot-axis and the old shoe shows nearly uniform
wear, the defect is not directly injurious. In very pronounced
" wryness," however, with thin, bent walls, a number of associated lesions, such as corns and cracks, may be present and
render the animal unfit for service upon paved or macadam
roads.

5. The Crooked Hoof.

A crooked hoof (Fig. 212) is one whose walls (viewed from
in front or behind) do not pass in a straight, natural direction
from the coronet to the ground, but are bent in such a manner
that the bearing-surface of the wall in relation to the foot axis
lies either too far out or in.

It may occur on any foot, but is seldom strongly marked.

Causes.—The causes are either long-continued leaving of one-half of the wall too high, or the use of shoes shaped for normal feet upon hoofs of the base-wide position.

The principal part of the treatment is the proper dressing of the hoof. The wall which is bent out at the middle and drawn in at the plantar border is, as a rule, too high and too near the centre of the foot (too narrow); the opposite wall, on the contrary, is too low and too far from the centre of the foot (too wide). This explains the manner in which the hoof should be cut down and rasped. The shoe must be laid out as far as possible towards the side which is too high and narrow. A straight edge placed against the high wall touches it only at its middle. The distance of this line from the lower edge of the wall shows us how far the surface of support— namely, the shoe—should be set out beyond the horn. If the straight edge be placed against the opposite wall, it will touch only at the coronet and at the plantar border, showing that the wall is concave. The distance of the middle of this wall from the straight edge shows us how much too wide this half of the wall is at its plantar border, and how much of the outer surface of the wall at its plantar border should be removed with the rasp. The restoration of a crooked hoof to its normal form requires several shoeings.

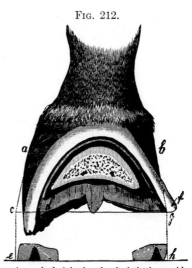

Fig. 212.

A crooked right fore-hoof of the base-wide position: *a*, convex wall, too high; *b*, concave wall, too low; *c d* shows how much of the outer wall must be removed with the hoof-knife; *f*, superfluous horn to be removed gradually with the rasp; *c e* and *g h* indicate the position of the shoe with relation to the hoof.

6. Ossification of the Lateral Cartilage (Side-Bone).

The ossification of a lateral cartilage (Fig. 213) consists in a change of the cartilage into bone. Heavy horses are more frequently affected than lighter ones. It most often involves the outer cartilages of the forefeet, seldom both cartilages. Side-bones always interfere with the physiological movements of the foot, and may, indeed, entirely suppress them.

The disease can only be diagnosed with certainty after the upper part of the cartilage has ossified. The coronet is then rather prominent (bulging), and feels hard. The gait is short and cautious, and well-marked lameness often follows severe work. As *causes,* may be mentioned predisposition in heavy lymphatic horses, and violent concussion or shock due to fast work upon hard roads. The disease is *incurable.*

FIG. 213.

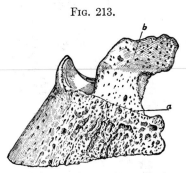

A left fore os pedis viewed in profile, showing ossification of the external lateral cartilage: *a,* dotted line shows normal line of union of cartilage with wing of os pedis; *b,* ossified portion ("side bone"). The unossified cartilage has been removed by maceration.

A special method of shoeing is only necessary when the outer cartilage is ossified and the quarter upon that side is contracted. After removing the old shoe, whose outer branch is, as a rule, more worn away than the inner, the outer wall will always be found too high, due to the fact that there has been little or no expansion and contraction in this quarter and, therefore, little or no wear of the horn against the shoe. The hoof is therefore wry,—on the outside too high, and on the inside too low. This shows us how the foot should be dressed so as to obtain a proper base of support and a uniform wear of the shoe. The most suitable shoe is a *flat shoe,* whose outer branch must be wider than the inner. It is so applied that the inner branch follows the edge of the wall closely, while the outer branch must be full and at the quarter must extend beyond the wall far enough to touch a perpendicular line dropped from the coronet (Fig. 215). The shoe must, therefore, be punched deep (coarse) on the outer branch and fine on the inner. A side-clip must be

FIG. 214.

Right fore-hoof whose form has changed as a result of ossification of the external lateral cartilage.

FIG. 215.

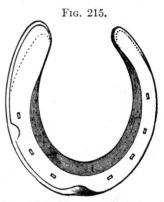

Shoe with broad outer branch, for the hoof shown in the preceding cut.

placed on the outer branch, because in time the outer half of the the hoof will again be too high. *Bar-shoes and rubber-pads are injurious when both cartilages are ossified,* but may be used when there is partial ossification of *but one cartilage,* especially if corns are present.

B. Disturbances of Continuity of the Hoof.

1. CRACKS.

Interruptions of continuity of the wall extending in the direction of the horn-tubes are known as cracks or seams. They have, according to their location, degree, and extent, not only various names, but also a varying significance.

Occurrence.—On the inner side of front hoofs, especially of horses that stand base-wide ; on hind hoofs, usually at the toe.

Classification.—According to location we distinguish toe-cracks, side-cracks, quarter-cracks, and bar-cracks. Those cracks which affect only the upper border of the hoof are called *coronary cracks;* those which are limited to the lower border of the hoof are sometimes designated *low cracks* (plantar cracks) ; while those which are continuous from one border to the other are called *complete cracks.* If the crack passes through the entire thickness of the wall to the sensitive tissues underneath,

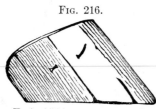

FIG. 216.

Hoof exhibiting a coronary crack, a plantar or low crack, and a complete deep crack, the latter with a nail ready to be clinched.

it is called a *deep or penetrating crack,* in contradistinction to the *superficial crack* (Fig. 216).

Causes.—There are many. Besides wounds of the coronet, everything that impairs the elasticity of the horn, weakens the hoof, and causes an overloading of one-half of the hoof. Furthermore, great dryness and excessive work on hard streets.

Prognosis.—This will depend upon the age, kind, and location of the crack. A *low crack is without significance* unless it is the remnant of an old coronary crack which has grown down. *Coronary cracks,* on the contrary, *are more serious* because of the lameness which often accompanies them, and especially on account of the long duration of the healing process.

The borders of the crack **never** grow together, and healing can only take place through healthy, unbroken horn growing down from the coronary band.

(*a*) *Treatment of Coronary and Bar-Cracks.*—If practicable, allow the affected horse to go barefoot; otherwise, the use of the **bar-shoe** for *all cracks* is advised, because it will continuously protect the diseased section of wall from pressure by the shoe. If there are present still other diseases of the hoof (corns, contraction, flat or full hoof), the addition of a leather sole with packing will be most beneficial, not only in favoring the healing of the crack, but also in improving the form of the hoof and in favoring the cure of the other lesions. In all coronary cracks it is of advantage to assist healing by fastening or immobilizing the borders of the crack by one of the following methods:

1. By rivets (nails), which pass across the crack through holes previously drilled in the horn (Fig. 217).

2. By clamps or hooks, which by means of special pincers are forced into pockets previously burnt into the horn on opposite sides of the crack (Fig. 219, B).

3. By a thin iron plate placed across the crack and secured by small screws, such as are used in wood (Figs. 220, 221).

4. By means of a bandage to last one shoeing.

Toe-crack occurs most often in draught-horses and most frequently in the hind feet. In shod hoofs it starts at the coronary border, and unless proper treatment is instituted soon reaches the plantar border. Long toes and low quarters and excessive dryness of the horn are predisposing causes. The exciting cause is usually forward pressure of the upper end of the short pastern against the thin upper edge of the wall of the toe. In the last part of the phase of contact of hoof with ground the pasterns are upright, or may even incline downward and backward (foot axis broken strongly backward), the short pastern presses the coronary band firmly against the upper thin edge of the toe, when if brittle through dryness it is unable to stretch and tears asunder. Thus, under the effort of starting a heavy load, when a horse with all four legs flexed has risen upon the points of his toes, a short quick slip followed by a catch, will frequently start a crack at the coronet.

The hoof should be so dressed and shod that the foot-axis shall be straight when seen from the side. In hind feet it is admissible to break the foot axis slightly forward. Therefore, shorten the toe and spare the quarters. If the latter are deficient in length, raise them by swelling the branches or by low heel-calks.

The shoe may be open, or a bar-shoe, or a short shoe with a rubber frog- and buttress-pad. Whatever expands the quarters closes a toe-crack. The Defay's shoe (Fig. 206), or the Chadwick spring beneath a rubber-pad, or beneath a bar-shoe with leather sole, if the frog be much shrunken, will be of service. The shoe should fit air-tight, except for an inch or so on both sides of the crack. Two lateral toe-clips (Fig. 217) are drawn up, and the wall between these clips is cut down from a twelfth to an eighth of an inch.

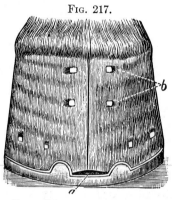

FIG. 217.

Toe-crack immobilized by lateral toe-clips: *a*, bearing-surface left free from pressure; *b*, heads of the rivets (nails) driven through holes previously drilled.

After the shoe has been nailed on tight the toe-crack should be immobilized. The best method is by buried nails. Slots are burned or cut on opposite sides at a distance of an inch from the crack. With a spiral drill (see Fig. 218) bore a hole from a slot at right angles to the

FIG. 218.

Spiral drill for boring the hole into which a round wire nail is driven to fasten a toe-crack. (*a*) three sided point of drill (similar to the point of a stilet of a cæcal trocar).

crack. Make a similar hole on the opposite side. Make the holes continuous by introducing a straight hot wire. The rivet may be an ordinary round wire nail which has been softened by bringing it to a yellow heat and allowing it to cool slowly.

It is driven through and the ends firmly clinched. Such a nail is easily placed, need not press upon fleshy leaves, can not be stripped off or lost, and holds fast. The horse should stand on the foot while the rivet is being clinched. Two are sufficient for a complete crack (Fig. 217).

A more rapid, though less efficient method of immobilizing a toe- or a quarter-crack is by the use of the Vachette hook. A special apparatus is required (see Fig. 219). The burning iron (Fig. 219, *A*) is brought to a yellow heat, its end applied to the wall so that the two ears are on opposite sides and equidistant from the crack, when it is pressed firmly till the shoulder (Fig. 219, *b*) touches the surface of the wall. A Vachette hook, the distance between the points of which equals the distance between the ears of the firing iron, is seized by the special pincers (*C*), pressed into the slots burned to receive it, and is then driven into the horn by compressing the pincers. At the toe these hooks are frequently stripped off by the heels of the opposite shoe (in hind feet). Free application of hoof ointment, and maceration of the horn by melting snow or mud tends to loosen them so that they often drop out.

An efficient method of fastening either a toe- or a quarter-crack is by using a metal plate one-sixteenth ($^1/_{16}''$) of an inch thick, provided with four to eight holes for the reception

Fig. 219.

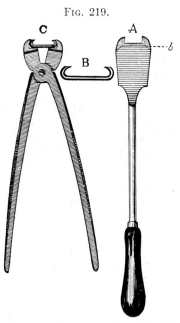

A, Vachette burning iron for making the two slots to receive the ends of the hook; *b*, shoulder; *B*, Vachette hook; *C*, pincers for forcing the hook into the wall.

of screws four- to five-sixteenths of an inch long. The plate is heated, bent to conform to the curvature of the wall and pressed against the horn till it burns a bed for itself, when it is screwed fast. It will not loosen (see Fig. 220, *b*). In every complete crack of the wall the growing down of coherent horn is favored by thinning the horn for an inch on both sides of the crack directly over the coronary band (see Fig. 221, *a*), so that any gliding movement between the sides of the crack below can

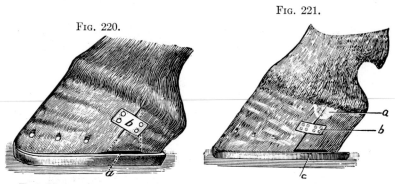

FIG. 220.

FIG. 221.

Hoof with coronary quarter-crack, shod with a bar-shoe. The part of the quarter relieved of pressure *a*, is indicated by the dotted lines; *b*, iron plate secured by small wood screws $\frac{4}{16}$–$\frac{5}{16}$ of an inch in length.

Hoof with complete quarter crack, shod with a bar-shoe: *a*, area thinned almost to the pododerm; *b*, $\frac{1}{13}$ inch metal plate secured by screw $\frac{5}{16}$ of an inch long; *c*, quarter relieved of pressure from bottom of crack to a perpendicular dropped from top of crack.

not be transmitted through the thinned area to the crack in the velvety tissue of the coronary band. Cutting a " V " at the coronet acts similarly, but is less efficient.

Quarter-crack is usually associated with contraction of the heels. It occurs on the inner quarter of base-wide (toe-wide) hoofs, and rarely in the outer quarter of base-narrow hoofs. For quarter-cracks we use a bar-shoe and determine the extent of the wall to be laid free in the following manner: We imagine the crack to be prolonged in the direction of the horn tubes to the plantar border, and drop a perpendicular line from the upper end of the crack to the plantar border. That part of the plantar border lying between these two points is then to be lowered sufficiently to prevent pressure from the shoe until the next shoeing (Figs. 220, *a,* and 221, *c*).

This method should be followed even when the perpendicular line falls behind the buttress.

The crack may be immobilized by the metal plate, or by narrow ticking bandage or adhesive tape wound a half dozen times around the hoof, in conjunction with a bar-shoe, Chadwick spring, leather sole and tar and oakum sole-packing.

In dressing the hoof, the side containing the crack should be spared, the opposite side lowered, the object being to shift the weight and consequent expansion into the sound quarter. When the affected quarter is deficient in length the branch of the shoe beneath should be made thicker, even to the extent of causing it to ground in advance of the opposite branch.

Next to shoeing, rubber hoof-pads render good service, because through them a part of the body-weight is distributed over the sole and frog. They assist in widening the hoof, and lessen shock when the foot is set to the ground. These are all matters which favor the growing down of unbroken horn.

When the crack gaps widely, and the frog is small and deep in the foot *a shoe with bar-clips* (Defay's shoe), or a Chadwick spring, with bar-shoe and leather sole may be used. It is not impossible, indeed, to obtain a cure by using an ordinary open flat shoe, though much will depend upon the other lesions that may be present, the nature of the hoof, and the service required of the animal.

If the edges of the crack are irregular and overlapping, they should be carefully thinned away. Thinning the horn on both sides of the crack over the coronary band, preventing drying out of the horn, and frequent applications of carbolized oil to the coronet favor growth of undivided horn and guard against a renewal of the crack.

If in the beginning of the disease there is inflammation and lameness, cooling poultices should be used for several days. When there is no lameness, the horse may be used for slow draft purposes. *Coach- and saddle-horses should be kept from fast work until sound horn has grown down at least one-half of an inch from the coronet.*

Bar-cracks are usually the result of changes of position of the quarters, and are just as frequently brought about by contraction as by leaving the quarters too high. We see them almost entirely upon the fore-hoofs. They seldom occur alone, but are usually accompanied by corns. When the crack extends to the pododerm there is a superficial inflammation of the pododerm and lameness. When treatment is not promptly begun the inflammation extends to the deeper layers of the pododerm, or, indeed, even to the plantar cushion, and gives rise to swelling of the bulb of the heel upon that side and to a well-marked lameness, which requires treatment by a competent veterinarian.

Ordinarily a bar-crack is only found by a close examination of the hoof after the shoe has been removed. In paring the hoof the crack usually appears as a dark streak, sometimes as a bloody fissure; not infrequently grayish hoof-pus is discovered in the depths of the crack.

The treatment must be directed towards favoring the growth of a continuous (unbroken) bar. This is accomplished by completely removing the edges of the crack, paring the horn of the vicinity very thin, and preventing the least pressure upon the wall of this quarter by the shoe, by lowering this quarter with the rasp and applying a **bar-shoe** with leather sole.

Following the removal of the edges of the crack there often appears, especially in stumpy hoofs, a deep groove; if the bottom of this groove is moist, we should pack it with oakum wet with a five per cent. solution of creolin or carbolic acid, and cover the oakum with wax (grafting wax). The cracks will return if the exciting causes cannot be completely removed.

(*b*) *Treatment of Low Cracks* (*Plantar Cracks*).—These cracks, occurring principally upon the hoofs of unshod horses, are the result of excessive stretching and bending of the lower border of the wall. Insufficient rounding of the wall with the rasp is largely responsible for them. An exciting cause in shod horses is the use of too large nails in shoes that are punched too fine.

Every coronary crack becomes in time a low or plantar crack, and this has an important bearing upon the prognosis, because a renewal of the coronary crack will be followed by a low crack.

In order to remove these cracks it is sufficient merely to shoe the horse. Upon shod horses they may be prevented by using properly punched shoes and thin nails. The lower border of the wall near the crack should be relieved of pressure by cutting out a half-moon-shaped piece of horn. To prevent the crack from extending farther upward we may burn a trans-verse slot at the upper end of the crack, in as far as the leafy layer of the wall, or cut such a slot with a small hoof-knife.

2. CLEFTS.

An interruption of continuity of the wall, at right angles to the direction of the horn-tubes, is called a *cleft*.

Clefts may occur at any part of the wall; yet they occur most often upon the inner toe and inner side, as a result of injury from sharp, improperly placed heel-calks (see page 173). How-ever, suppurating corns, or other suppurative processes situated at the coronet or which find their point of escape at the coronet, may from time to time lead to separa-tions of continuity and the forma-tion of horn-clefts.

FIG. 222.

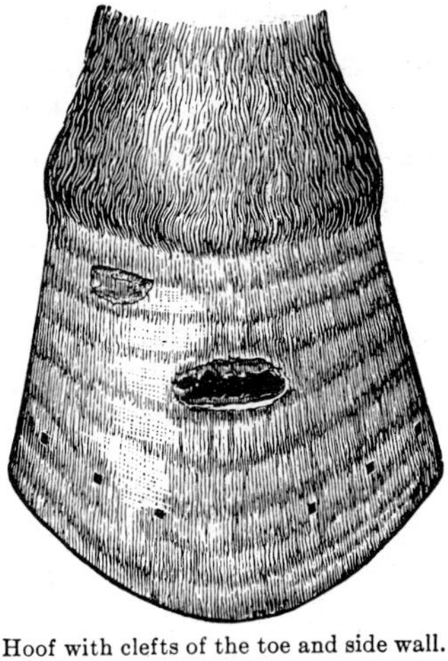

Horn-clefts, though the result of lesions which are often very injurious and interefere with the use of the horse, are of themselves not an evil which can be abolished

Hoof with clefts of the toe and side wall.

or healed by shoeing, although, in many cases, proper shoeing would have prevented them. A horn-cleft is not a matter for consideration by the shoer until it has grown down so far that it comes within the region of the nails.

In order not to disfigure the hoof unnecessarily, the horn below the cleft should be kept in place as long as possible by shortening the wall at that point, to remove shoe-pressure, and by driving no nails into it. If, however, the horn is loose and about to come away, it should be removed and the defect filled with Defay's patent horn-cement.

3. Loose Wall.

Separation of the wall from the sole *in the white line* is called loose wall (Fig. 223, *a*).

Occurrence.—Frequent on the fore-hoofs of shod and un-shod horses, and oftener upon the inner than upon the outer side. More rare on hind hoofs. Common-bred horses with wide and flat feet are predisposed to this trouble.

We distinguish *superficial* and *deep loose wall;* only the latter requires the shoer's attention, because it leads to lameness.

Causes.—Walls which are very oblique (slanting); outward bendings of the plantar border of the wall; burning the horn with hot shoes; dryness; neglected shoeing; excessive softening of the horn with poultices, particularly of cow-dung; careless-ness in preparing the bearing-surfaces of hoof and shoe in shoe-ing; uneven fitting of the shoe.

Treatment.—It aims to remove the lameness and to favor growth of coherent horn. In the first place the removal of the exciting causes, followed by proper shortening of the wall. We should apply a shoe whose bearing-surface *inclines slightly down-ward and inward,* is perfectly smooth, and wide enough to cover the wall, white line, and outer border of the sole; the iron should be only moderately warm. Where there is lameness we use a leather sole with packing, or a **bar-shoe.** The loose wall should be freed from shoe-pressure only when it does not extend far along the white line. When the separation is extensive the loose wall should not be lowered. The crack should be filled with wood-tar, crude turpentine, or soft grafting-wax.

If a loose wall occur upon the foot of a horse while running barefoot, all separated horn should be removed; if, on account of the nature of the ground, this seems to be impracticable, the hoof must be shod.

Care of the Hoof.—Shoe at least every four to five weeks. Preserve the pliancy and toughness of the horn by judicious moistening.

4. Hollow Wall.

A *hollow wall is one in which a separation has occurred between the middle layer of the wall and the keraphyllous layer.* This crack or separation always extends in the direction of the layers of the wall (Fig. 223, *b*).

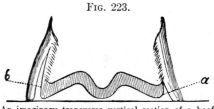

FIG. 223.

An imaginary transverse vertical section of a hoof showing (*a*) loose wall and (*b*) hollow wall.

Occurrence.—Quite rare.

We should suspect a hollow wall when a part of the wall *rounds out prominently beyond the rest,* and gives forth a hollow (resonant) sound when struck. The white line presents a crack, yet we should hesitate to form a conclusion as to the extent of the separation from the extent of the crack along the white line, since the latter may be considerably smaller. The separation extends higher up the wall than in the case of loose wall, frequently to the coronet. The cavity is usually filled with crumbling, disintegrated horn.

Hollow wall is not often accompanied by pain. Lameness may arise, however, if the hollow section of wall assists in bearing the body-weight, and if the animal does fast work upon paved streets.

Causes.—Mechanical influences resulting in chronic inflammation of fleshy leaves.

Treatment.—A cure is possible, but requires considerable time. In shoeing, which should always aim to *relieve pressure* from the hollow section of wall, we cleanse the cavity and fill it with oakum and tar, crude turpentine, or wax. Where the separation is very extensive we use a *bar-shoe.*

The time required for complete cure of hollow and loose walls will depend upon the height of the separation (see growth of the hoof, page 82).

5. THRUSH OF THE FROG.

When the horny frog is ragged and fissured, and an ill-smelling, dark-colored liquid collects in the lacunæ of the frog, it is affected with thrush. When thrush exists uninterruptedly for several months the perioplic band is irritated and forms rings of periople which assume an irregular course and cross the rings of the middle layer of the wall (Fig. 224).

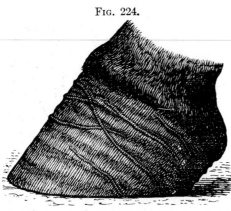

FIG. 224.

Hoof with irregular superficial rings resulting from thrush of the frog.

The *causes:* un-cleanliness, **too little exercise** in fresh air, excessive paring of the frog, and the use of shoes with calks by which the frog is permanently removed from the ground.

The *consequences* are, besides contraction of the hoof, soreness in travelling, a shortening of the step, and, occasionally, well-marked lameness.

Treatment.—Removal of all greasy horn from the frog, and of the prominent overgrown angles of the buttresses (see page 100), thorough washing of the frog once or twice daily with a 5 per cent. creolin or carbolic solution, **abundant exercise,** and shoes without calks.

CHAPTER X.

SHOEING MULES, ASSES, AND OXEN.

1. The shoeing of mules and asses is, as in the case of horses, a necessity if these animals are to be used for draft or saddle purposes on hard streets. The structure and characteristics of the hoofs of these animals are quite similar to those of the horse, differing chiefly in the form and thickness of the wall. The mule hoof is long and narrow and round at the toe, the sole is well arched, and the side walls are rather steep (Fig. 225). In the ass the narrowness of hoof is still more pronounced, the wall is relatively **thick,** the frog is particularly well developed in its branches, and therefore the hoof is relatively wide in the region of the quarters. The horn of both mule and ass is tough.

FIG. 225.

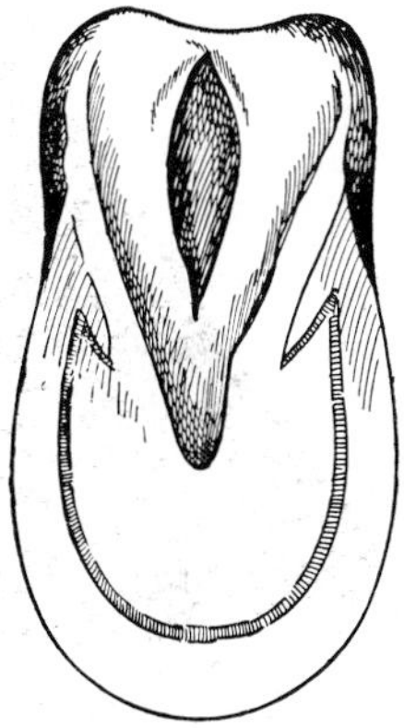

A mule's hoof. (Plantar surface).

The shoes differ from those of the horse in no other respect than that they should be lighter and narrower. Four nail-holes are sufficient for an ass' shoe, and five to six for a mule's.

On account of the hardness and toughness of the walls, we use nails that are short but strong in the shank; nails with weak shanks are apt to bend in driving.

2. *The shoeing of oxen* is essentially different from that of horses, because the foot of the ox is cloven (split), the long pastern, short pastern, and hoof-bone are double, so that, instead of one hoof or claw, there are two upon each foot, distinguished as outer and inner. Each claw consists of wall,

207

sole, and bulbs; the frog is absent. The wall is considerably thinner than that of the horse's hoof, the sole is thin, and the bulbs are low. For these reasons the shoe designed for a claw must be thin, but wide.

The holes must be punched fine and the nails be quite short and strong. On each shoe a long tongue should be made on the inner edge near the toe, and so directed that it can be turned upward and outward to embrace the toe of the claw.

Fig. 226.

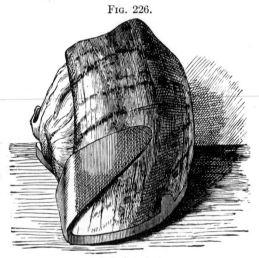

A shod ox-claw.

A small clip raised on the outer toe of each shoe will increase its stability. In some parts of Saxony the shoes are so made that the tongue of each shoe begins in the rear third of its inner edge and runs forward, upward, and outward, closely embracing the wall of the toe. The smaller clip is drawn up on the outer edge of the shoe close to the toe. These shoes are more difficult to make, but when applied sit more firmly and remain fast longer than all others. Machine-made ox shoes (Fig. 227) have no clip at the inner toe, and are fre-

quently pulled and lost. For this reason they are inferior to
hand-made shoes. An undivided shoe (the so-called " closed
claw-shoe ") is unsuitable for oxen, because it deprives both
claws of their natural, free movements. However, such a shoe
is of advantage for heavy draft over hard and very rough
roads, because it lessens the liability of the fetlock and coronary
joints and the cleft of the claws to strains.

Great difficulty is often encountered in holding the feet
during the operation of shoeing. It is necessary to fasten the
head securely against a tree,
post, or wall. A front foot
may be raised and held by
passing a slip-noose in the
end of a rope or side-line
around the fetlock and carrying the line over the withers
to the opposite side, where it
is held by an assistant. A
hind limb may be controlled
by passing a round pole in
front of the hock of the leg
to be raised, and, with a man
at each end of the pole, carrying the limb backward and
upward, in which position it

FIG. 227.

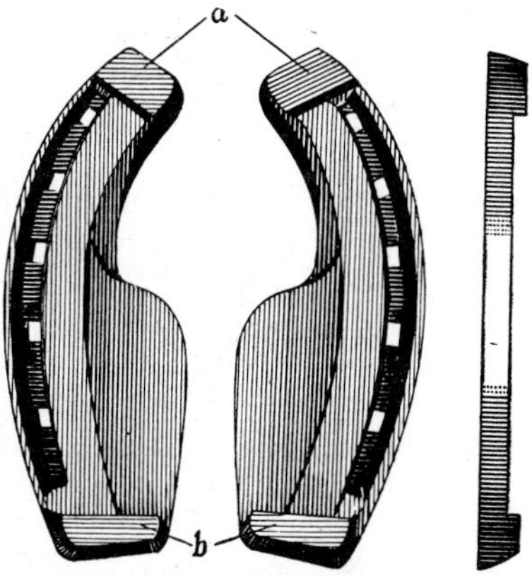

Pair of machine made ox shoes, viewed from
the ground-surface and in profile; *a*, toe-calk; *b*,
heel-calks.

is held; or the limb may be bent and controlled by tightening a
twitch or tourniquet upon the leg just above the hock (Fig.
228). Oxen that continue to resist may sometimes be quieted
by light blows of a short stick upon the base of the horns. In
parts of the country where many oxen are shod stocks are in
common use.

Very satisfactory stocks have been designed by Gutenaecker,
of Munich (Fig. 229). The four corner-posts (*a, a, b, b*) are
eight inches square and eight feet long, of which three feet

four inches are solidly implanted in the ground. They are
united by side- and cross-bars (c, c, d). In front of the corner-
posts (a, a) and in the middle line stands a head-post (e) of
the same dimensions as the corner-posts, provided with a slot
four inches wide and twenty inches long beginning three feet
from the ground. In this slot is a pulley-wheel (i), and below
it a windlass (k) for winding up the rope which is tied around
the base of the animal's horns. The corner-posts are provided
with a slot (n) three inches wide and three inches deep,

FIG. 228.

Hind foot raised by means of a round pole.

within which are placed two movable side-bars (o, p), which
can be set at desired heights and fastened by iron pins. Between the front and rear corner-posts of the right-hand side is
an eight-sided roller with a ratchet and click at one end, and
having on one of the sides six iron hooks, to which a girth is
attached. On the opposite side of the stocks, at the same
height, is a stationary bar (f) with six hooks (g, g) on the
outer side. The belly girth is six feet long, six inches wide,
and terminates at both ends in several strong cords two feet

four inches long with iron rings at their ends. Between the front corner-posts are a neck-yoke (*h*) and a breast-bar which

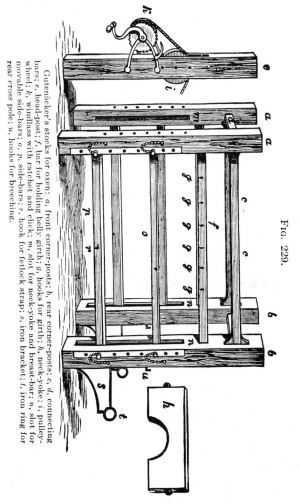

Fig. 229.

Gutenäcker's stocks for oxen: *a*, front corner-posts; *b*, rear corner-posts; *c*, *d*, connecting bars; *e*, head-post; *f*, bar for holding belly girth; *g*, hooks for girth; *h*, neck-yoke; *i*, pulley-wheel; *k*, windlass with ratchet and click; *m*, slot for neck-yoke and breast-bar; *n*, slot for movable side-bars; *o*, *p*, side-bars; *r*, hook for fetlock strap; *s*, iron bracket; *t*, iron ring for rear cross pole; *u*, hooks for breeching.

slide in the slots (*m*) and may be fixed at desired heights by iron pins. On the rear face of each rear corner-post is an iron bracket (*s*) one foot and a half long, with a ring (*t*) six inches in diameter, through which passes a round pole padded in the middle and kept in place by two iron pins. Above each bracket is a hook (*u*) to which the end of the breeching attaches.

Before an animal is brought into the stocks the neck-yoke is raised, the breast-bar lowered, and the girth left hanging from the hooks on the stationary bar. The ox is then led into the stocks and the rope which is tied around the base of the horns is carried over the pulley (*i*), fastened to the hook on the roller (*k*), and wound up till the head is tight against the head-post. The yoke and breast-bar are then placed in position and fastened, the breeching hung on the hooks (*u*), and the belly girth attached to the hooks on the roller, so that, if need be, it can be shortened till it bears the animal's entire weight.

To control a front foot a slip noose is placed about the fetlock and the limb is raised and lashed to the side-bar, the rope passing finally to the hook (*r*). To control a hind foot a slip noose is placed about the fetlock, the foot carried upward and backward over the rear cross-bar, and, with the front surface of the fetlock-joint resting against the padding of the bar, the limb is firmly secured by wrapping the line several times about the limb and bar.

When no stocks are at hand, we may use an ordinary farm wagon or a truck wagon. Tie the ox with his head forward between the front and hind wheels. Fasten the large end of a binding pole to the spokes of the front wheel and let it rest on the hub. Swing the pole close to the ox and induce him to step over it with one hind leg, then raise the rear end of the pole, and with it the leg and so much of the animal's hind quarters that the inner hind leg standing close to the wagon rests but lightly upon the ground. The binding pole may then be slung with a rope from the rack of the wagon or other stationary object and the outer limb held in the usual manner. By following this method a shoer with one assistant can easily and safely control the most refractory oxen.

INDEX

213